AIR FRYER COOKBOOK 2023 UK

1200 Days of Quick & Easy British Air Fryer Recipes for Beginners and Advanced

NAOMI LANE

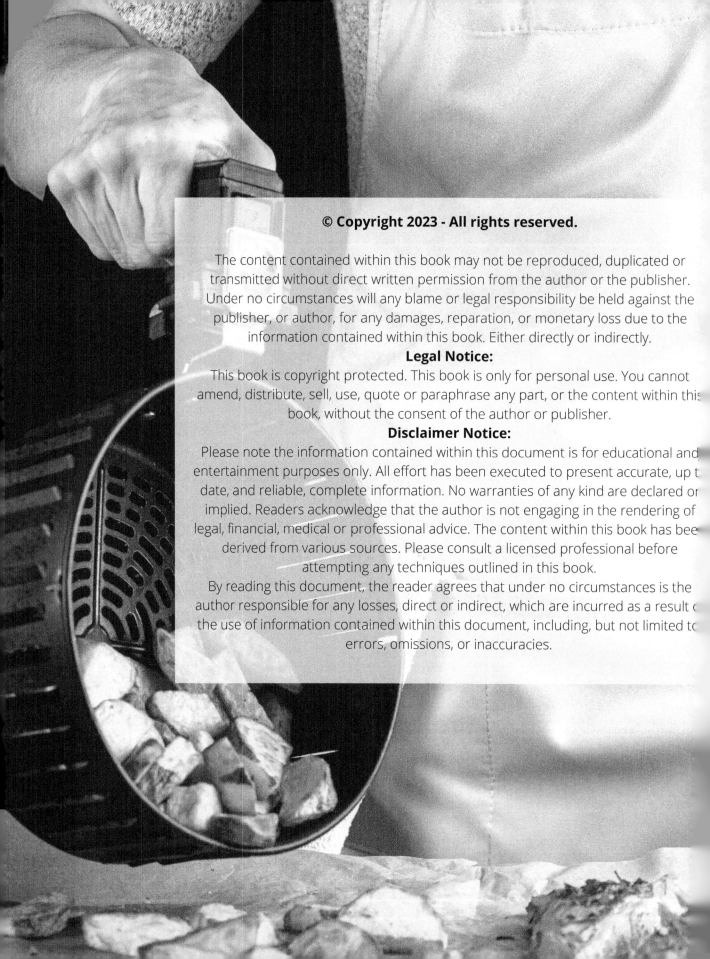

TABLE OF CONTENT

i

INTRODUCTION

We all know the fantastic taste of deep-fried foods. The mere mention of deep-fried beef burgers, French fries, and chicken drumsticks is mouth-watering. Whether you are a home cook or a skilful chef, you will concur that deep-frying food is one of the efficient, convenient, and most used cooking methods.

However, we can't deny that deep-fried food is unhealthy. They are highly packed with calories and fat that significantly affect our health. Also, deep-frying ingredients lose vital nutrients and, even worse, expose our bodies to the risk of cancer, obesity, and diabetes despite their flavourful taste.

Fortunately, the cooking revolution began with the introduction of the air fryer. You can now cook crunchy, crispy meals without compromising flavour, the big clean-up, and expenses associated with deep frying. You can achieve better results since your food is super crisp with little or no oil.

The promise of this kitchen gadget is simple; Crunchy, healthy food. It can make guilt-free French fries, nachos, and lamb roasts in half the time you make them in the oven. It can also cook strip steak in less time than it takes to preheat a grill and can reheat leftovers producing better results than your microwave.

Too good to be true. Right? This cookbook is going to be your torchbearer. It will guide you into understanding and mastering how the air fryer works, tips and tricks for using it, troubleshooting it, and delicious recipes for almost every occasion with easy-to-follow steps and beautiful photos of the result. What are you waiting for? Let's go!

An air fryer is an amped-up small countertop convection oven that stimulates deep frying food without submerging them in oil. It cooks food using heating elements accompanied by a powerful fan that circularly swirls hot air in the cooking chamber. The hot air reaches the ingredients creating a crispy crust on the outside and a moist inside.

The perforated basket makes an air fryer so good at its job. This is where the food sits. The perforations help increase the contact between food and the moving hot air.

Let's have an overview of how to use an air fryer.

1. **Place the food in the perforated basket.**

   The size of the basket varies with the air fryer size. The basket may hold 2-10 quarts of ingredients. Adding 1-2 tablespoons of oil is recommended to achieve fried foods' crunchiness.

2. **Set the desired time and temperature**

   Air fryer times range from 5-25 minutes, while the temperature ranges from 350 F-400F.

3. **Give the food time to cook.**

   Flipping the food halfway through the cooking time is highly recommended, which helps the food crisp up evenly.

Benefits of using the air fryer

1. **May aid weight loss**

   The key to successful weight loss is watching the eating and cooking habits. The air fryer reduces calorie intake and may contribute to weight loss. Besides, the air fryer uses a tablespoon or no oil, thus decreasing fattening cholesterol intake.

2. **Safe to use.**

   Unlike deep frying, which involves heating a large amount of oil that may spill or splash, posing an accident, the air fryer uses little or no oil. The air fryer comes with auto shutdown features when the cooking cycle is complete, preventing it from overheating and burning. Even better, the air fryer has non-slip feet that ensure the appliance doesn't slip when cooking causing accidents.

3. **Cooks food faster**

   Foods cook fast in the air fryer than in other kitchen appliances such as the oven. The air fryers also do not require preheating before cooking commences. Most importantly, you may transfer frozen ingredients straight to the air fryer from the freezer.

4. **Perfect for veggies picky eaters**

   Air frying vegetables such as broccoli, kale, or Brussels sprouts are great solutions for picky vegetable eaters. The veggies come out crispy and tastier, thus irresistible. Moreover, some air fryer recipes allow breading of the vegetables before air frying incorporating healthy options such as chickpeas and rice crumbs.

5. **Easy to clean**

   Not only is it easy to cook with an air fryer but also to clean. Most of the removable components of the air fryer are dishwasher safe. You can also soak them in warm soapy water or wipe them with a damp cloth.

6. **It takes less of your kitchen space.**

   This is a perfect kitchen appliance for you if you have a small kitchen space. It takes up less of the countertop space and is sleek, thus a great addition to the kitchen. The air fryer also doesn't leave your house with fried food smells that last for hours after cooking.

Tips and tricks of using the air fryer

An air fryer can be a great addition to your kitchen if you use it in the right way. Below are some tips to help you exploit its full potential.

Preparing to Air Fry

1. Ensure that your air fryer is placed on a stable, level countertop that is heat resistant. You should also leave at least 13 centimetres distance between a surface and the air fryer exhaust vent.

2. It's unnecessary, but it is advisable to preheat the air fryer before adding the ingredients. Set the timer for 2-3 minutes, and add food immediately after the timer stops.

3. Invest in a hand-pumped kitchen cooking spray bottle. Spraying oil on the food is better than brushing or drizzling. Less oil is used and reaches the ingredients evenly. However, be aware of oil cans with aerosol agents that can corrode your air fryer basket's non-stick surface.

4. Use an aluminium sling to remove the air fryer's hot cooking accessories. Fold a piece of aluminium foil into about 21/2" wide and 25 long slings. Please place it in the air fryer and the baking dish, then tuck the ends in the basket. Once the cooking cycle is complete, untuck the sling and lift the baking dish.

5. Invest in the right air fryer accessories. You may purchase brand new ones or may already have some. Let's say, for example; you have an oven-safe baking dish. It can also be used in the air fryer as long as it fits in the appliance and doesn't touch the heating element.

6. If your recipe involves breading, make sure to use the proper breading technique. Coat the ingredients with flour, then dip in the egg and crumbs. Press the crumbs using your hands to ensure the fan does not brown them off.

When Air Frying

1. Fatty foods, e.g., bacon and meat burgers, produce grease that tends to smoke when too hot. Therefore, add cold water to the drawer below the air fryer basket to prevent the oil from getting hot and smoking.

2. As you would when cooking on the stovetop, grill, or skillet, flip food halfway through the cooking cycle. You can also shake the air fryer basket to

distribute the ingredients well during the cooking cycle. This helps crisping, browning, and cooking evenly.

3. We tend to overcrowd the skillet or other cooking appliances, so why not the air fryer? I can't stress this enough. Overcrowding the basket to cook more at a time will prevent food from cooking and crisping well.

4. Unlike some cooking appliances, you can check the food doneness as often as required and as you like. This is the most exciting part of using the air fryer since you don't interrupt the timing. Some air fryer models continue heating even when the drawer is open, while others pick from where it left off once the drawer is returned.

5. Secure light food like the top bun on a sandwich with a toothpick to avoid being blown around by the powerful fan.

6. Spray your food halfway through the cooking cycle to get it brownier and crispier

7. Cook food without overlapping. This helps plenty of air circulation, attributing to even cooking. However, you can stack vegetables, e.g. Brussels sprouts, and flip them a few times during the cooking process.

8. Always use a meat thermometer to ensure the meat browns nicely on the outside and reach the inside's proper temperature.

After Air frying

1. Remove the air fryer basket from the drawer before pouring food on a serving platter. This prevents you from pouring excess grease and fat alongside the air-fried food.

2. Do not pour the cooking juices from the drawer just yet. The drawer catches marinade from cooking food packed with flavour and may be used as a serving sauce. If the liquid is too thin, boil it over the stovetop until it thickens. You may also add cornstarch and cook it over the stovetop for a few minutes to thicken. Serve the air-fried food with the gravy.

3. After using the air fryer, clean the basket and the drawer with warm soapy water. Return the accessories and turn on the air fryer for 3 minutes to dry itself. This ensures the accessories are well dried compared to using towels.

Valuable tools to exploit all potential of the air fryer

Did you just purchase your first air fryer? Are you wondering what to do with it? If either or both questions answer yes, here are essential accessories to get you started with your air fryer. The tools will make it easy for you to make almost everything in your air fryer.

Silicone locking tongs

Tongs are used to move food in and out of the air fryer, protecting your fingers and arms from burns. Ensure the tongs are flexible, heat resistant, dishwasher safe, stainless, and have silicon heads to grip food easily.

Air fryer liners

Invest in non-stick and non-toxic air fryer liners. They prevent food from sticking and keep fatty residue out, making cleaning a breeze.

Reversible Air fryer Rack

Air fryers perform great work circulating air around your food in the air fryer. However, large foods such as beef roast or chicken drumsticks will require an elevation so that the air can circulate them evenly instead of leaving one side of the food to lie on the air fryer's bottom. Even better, some racks come with skewers for vegetable or meat kabobs and peach bourbon wings. The frame is also dishwasher safe, thus easy to clean up.

Air fryer Silicon Cups

The reusable silicone cups create muffins, cupcakes, or egg cups. They help develop batches of similar or personalised foods in the air fryer.

Air fryer grill pan

When cooking fish or other meat, an air fryer grill pan is a convenient tool you must have. It comes with a perforated surface to allow air circulation. It is also non-stick and dishwasher safe for easy cleaning.

Air fryer baking pan

As aforementioned, the air fryer resembles a convection oven, thus great for baking. The baking pan fits in the air fryer and can cook all sorts of baked foods ranging from cakes, bread, and eggs with vegetables, macaroni and cheese, and pizza, among others.

Mandoline slicer

Do you love air-fried French fries, onion rings, or sliced pickles? Mandoline is the one for you. This pull and slice equipment have different thickness settings per the recipe requirement. Remember to follow mandoline safety precautions to avoid injuries.

Spray Bottle

Spraying your food is the secret to crispier and brownier food in the air fryer. It's also economical to pour oil compared to brushing or drizzling oil on the food. We earlier stated that some oil cans contain aerosol agents that can dissipate your air fryer coating. Right? Fill a spray bottle with your favourite oil before air frying for an excellent food outcome and a lasting relationship with your air fryer.

Meat Thermometer

Correct cooking times and food temperatures are the keys to successful air frying. A meat thermometer ensures your food is cooked up to the proper temperatures. The thermometer can read the food temperatures within seconds and be folded and stored anywhere.

Maintenance and troubleshooting

You were excited that you finally got your dream magical kitchen appliance. You even told your friends and invited them to your place to witness how you are now making and eating healthy. You feel very proud of yourself and can't ask for more. Sadly, after some time, the air fryer doesn't work right. There must be something wrong with it. You are now wondering how to deal with it and get your air fryer back on track. Below are some problems common with air fryers and their solutions.

Problem: The smell of old food
Remedy:

Foods with strong smells, such as fish or bacon, may leave an odour in your air fryer. The perfect way to deal with the odours is to clean the air fryer immediately after you are done cooking. If the smell persists, soak the basket and the drawer in warm soapy water for about an hour, and clean them again. Suppose that doesn't work half a lemon and rub the halves over the accessories. Let sit for half an hour and wash with soapy water. The air fryer should now be clean and smell fresh.

Problem: The air fryer won't switch on or off
Remedy:

This is a common issue among many air fryers and is the easiest to fix. The air fryer's main reason for failing to switch on is a wrongly plugged power source. Counter-check the air fryer connection and fit it well. Another main reason is an overloaded socket limiting the amount of power reaching your gadget. If this is the case, unplug some devices from the socket; otherwise, use an alternative idle socket for the air fryer.

Problem: White Smoke
Remedy:

White smoke is mostly not smoke but natural steam when cooking moist food. If the smoke has a smell, unplug the air fryer immediately. Check if accumulated grease is on the drip pan from cooking fatty foods. Let the air fryer cool and wash the oil if that is the case.

Problem: Black smoke
Remedy:

Black smoke results from cooking fatty foods at high temperatures. The smoke may produce an odour of burning fat. You can prevent this by adding a small amount of water to the basket's bottom, where hot oil will land and cool.

Problem: Blue smoke
Remedy:

Blue smoke is exceptionally rare but a cause for concern. If it does happen, it means that there is an electric problem. You should act fast, unplug the air fryer, and don't plug it back in until a technician attends. If you don't desire to repair the air fryer consider purchasing a new air fryer.

Problem: Food lacks a crispy finish
Remedy:

The lack of a crispy texture in your air fried is commonly observed when your food cooks with air instead of oil. Always spray cooking spray on the ingredients before air frying.

Problem: Improperly cooked food
Remedy:

This is a common predicament among many air fryer users. It's mainly caused by overloading the basket and the hot air not reaching all the food. This can be solved by cooking small batches of food and shaking the basket regularly to help distribute heat evenly.

Problem: Air fryer not blowing hot air
Remedy:
Failure of an air fryer to blow hot air is a fault that the manufacturer or the outlet where you bought the appliance should be repaired. If your warranty has not yet expired, ensure to get a repair service.

Problem: producing too much noise
Remedy:

If your air fryer is making a rattling noise, it's likely an accessory or a part inside that is not well fitted. You can correct this by switching it off and cleaning it while inspecting if any tightening is needed in the interior. Moreover, if the fan is moving at a very high speed, it is likely to make noise as loud as the noise made by a vacuum.

Problem: Air fryer peeling
Remedy:

If your air fryer's non-stick surface starts to peel weeks or a month after purchase, it is a call for action. You may be using abrasive cleaning equipment or using a can of oil with aerosol agents. Prevent such incidents by cleaning the air fryer with a soft sponge and purchasing a spray bottle.

1. Air Fryer Frittata

Preparation Time:
15 minutes

Cooking time:
20 minutes

Serving:
2

INGREDIENTS

- Cooking spray
- 113g fully cooked and crumbled sausage
- 4 eggs, beaten
- 120g cheddar-Monterey jack cheese blend, shredded
- 2 tbsp diced green bell pepper
- 1 chopped green onion
- 1 pinch cayenne pepper

DIRECTIONS

1. Preheat the air fryer to 180°C and spray a cake pan with cooking spray.
2. Mix all the ingredients in a bowl until they are well combined.
3. Transfer the mixture in the bowl to the cake pan.
4. Cook the frittata for 20 minutes.
5. Transfer the frittata to a serving platter.
6. Serve and enjoy.

 Nutrition- Per Serving:
Calories 381kcal, Total Fat: 27g, Carbs: 3g, Proteins 31g

 Variation:
The sausage can be replaced with leftover steak.

---

2. Air Fryer Blueberry Muffins

Preparation Time:
10 minutes

Cooking time:
15 minutes

Serving:
12

INGREDIENTS

- 187g all-purpose flour
- 53g oatmeal
- ½ tbsp salt
- ½ tbsp cinnamon
- 97g brown sweetener
- 1 tbsp baking powder

- 118ml of milk
- 2 eggs, beaten
- 2 tbsp vanilla
- 57g unsalted butter, melted
- 190g blueberries

DIRECTIONS

1. Mix the flour, oatmeal, salt, cinnamon, brown sweetener, and baking powder in a bowl.
2. Whisk the milk, eggs, vanilla, and butter in a separate bowl.
3. Stir in the dry ingredients to the wet ingredients.
4. Add the blueberries to the batter and mix.
5. Preheat the air fryer to 177°C.
6. Transfer the batter to 12 silicone muffin cups.
7. Cook the muffins for 15 minutes.
8. Serve and enjoy.

 Nutrition- Per Serving:
   Calories 11kcal, Total Fat: 11g, Carbs: 11g, Proteins 11g

 Variation:
   Brown sugar can be used instead of brown sweetener.
   Fresh or frozen blueberries can be used depending on your preference.

3. Air Fryer Sweet Potato Skins

Preparation Time:
7 minutes

Cooking time:
23 minutes

Serving:
4

INGREDIENTS

- 2 sweet potatoes
- 2 tbsp olive oil
- Salt to taste
- 4 eggs, beaten
- 59ml whole milk

- pepper to taste
- 4 bacon slices, cooked
- 59g cheddar cheese, grated
- 2 sliced green onions

DIRECTIONS

1. Wash the sweet potatoes and cook them in a microwave for 8 minutes until they are soft.
2. Wear the oven mitt and slice the sweet potatoes lengthwise into halves.
3. Scoop most of the sweet potato flesh leaving 2 ½ cm thick flesh.
4. Brush the sweet potato skins with oil and sprinkle them with salt.
5. Preheat the air fryer to 204**°**C.
6. Place the sweet potato skins in the air fryer and cook them for 10 minutes.
7. Meanwhile, mix the eggs, milk, salt, and pepper in a skillet.
8. Cook the egg mixture for about 2 minutes over medium heat, stirring constantly.
9. Top the sweet potato skins with 2 spoonfuls of the egg mixture and 1 slice of bacon.
10. Cover the sweet potato with cheese and cook in the air fryer for 3 minutes.
11. Garnish the sweet potato skins with green onion and serve.

 Nutrition- Per Serving:
Calories 207kcal, Total Fat: 12g, Carbs: 15g, Proteins 11g

 Variation:
The desired type of cheese can be used.

---

4. Air Fryer Omelette

Preparation Time:
2 minutes

Cooking time:
10 minutes

Serving:
4

INGREDIENTS

- 2 eggs, beaten
- 59ml milk
- Salt to taste
- 57g fresh meat, minced
- ½ red bell pepper, diced
- 1 green onion, diced
- 118g fresh mushroom, diced
- 4 tbsp garden herb
- 59g mozzarella cheese, shredded

DIRECTIONS

1. Whisk the eggs and milk in a bowl.
2. Stir in salt, meat, and veggies to the egg mixture.
3. Pour the egg mixture into a greased pan.
4. Place the pan in an air fryer basket and cook at 177ºC for about 5 minutes.
5. Sprinkle the garden herb onto the omelette, then sprinkle it with cheese.
6. Cook the omelette for 5 minutes.
7. Transfer the omelette to a serving platter.

8. Serve and enjoy.

 Nutrition- Per Serving:

Calories 106kcal, Total Fat:6g, Carbs: 5g, Proteins 10g

 Variation:
The garden herb can be replaced with the desired seasoning.

---

5. Air Fryer Sausage and Cheese wraps

Preparation Time:
5 minutes

Cooking time:
6 minutes

Serving:
8

INGREDIENTS

- 8 Heat N' Serve sausage
- 2 pieces of cheese, sliced
- 8 refrigerated crescent roll dough
- 8 wooden skewers

DIRECTIONS

1. Separate the crescent roll dough into triangles on a flat surface.
2. Place one triangle on a flat surface and place the sausage and cheese on the edge of the widest part of the dough.
3. Roll the dough over the sausage and cheese and pin the seam to seal.
4. Preheat the air fryer to 193°C.
5. Air fry the sausage wraps in batches for 3 minutes.
6. Add the sausage wraps in skewers and serve.

 Nutrition- Per Serving:
Calories 125kcal, Total Fat: 6g, Carbs: 16g, Proteins 5g

 Variation: American cheese can be replaced with the desired cheese.

---

6. Air Fryer Cinnamon Rolls

Preparation Time:
10 minutes

Cooking time:
10 minutes

Serving:
10

INGREDIENTS

- 75g melted butter
- 64g brown sugar
- 2 tbsp maple syrup
- 39g walnuts, chopped
- 53g raisins
- 1 tbsp cinnamon
- 2 tbsp brown sugar
- 1 crescent roll, refrigerated

DIRECTIONS

1. In a bowl, whisk butter, sugar, and maple syrup.
2. Brush an air fryer-safe pan with oil.
3. Pour the sugar mixture into the pan, then sprinkle it with walnuts and raisins.
4. In a separate bowl, mix the cinnamon and sugar.
5. Cut the crescent roll into 8 pieces without unrolling them.
6. Dip the crescent rolls in the cinnamon mixture, then place them in the pan.
7. Air fry the cinnamon rolls at 173°C for 10 minutes, flipping them halfway during cooking.
8. Transfer the rolls to a serving platter, then spoon the mixture into the pan on top of the rolls.
9. Serve and enjoy.

 Nutrition- Per Serving:
Calories 143kcal, Total Fat:8g, Carbs: 18g, Proteins 2g

 Variations: Walnuts can be replaced with pecans.

---

7. Air Fryer Avocado and Egg Pizza Toast

Preparation Time:
10 minutes

Cooking time:
10 minutes

Serving:
4

INGREDIENTS

- 4 bread slices, trimmed
- 53g mayonnaise
- 117g cheddar cheese, shredded
- 1 thinly sliced avocado
- 3 eggs
- Salt and black pepper to taste

- 59g mozzarella cheese, shredded

DIRECTIONS

1. Preheat the air fryer to 204°C and lightly brush the baking pan with cooking spray.
2. Place the bread slices on the pan.
3. Spread ¾ of the mayonnaise on the bread slices, then sprinkle them with ¾ cheddar cheese.
4. Fill the wall and centre of the pan with the avocado slices so the pizza will look like a peace symbol with 3 compartments.
5. Crack each egg onto each compartment and spread the remaining mayonnaise over the eggs.
6. Sprinkle the avocado with salt, pepper, and the remaining cheddar cheese.
7. Place the pan in the air fryer and cook for 7 minutes.
8. Sprinkle the mozzarella on the pizza and cook it for an additional 3 minutes.
9. Serve and enjoy.

 Nutrition- Per Serving:
Calories 302kcal, Total Fat: 28g, Carbs: 4g, Proteins 10g

 Variation: The desired cheese can be used.

---

8. Air Fryer Pancakes

Preparation Time:
10 minutes

Cooking time:
10 minutes

Serving:
4

INGREDIENTS

- 188g all-purpose flour
- 3½ tbsp baking powder
- 1 ½ tbsp baking soda
- 1 tbsp salt
- 1 tbsp sugar
- 296ml milk
- 1 egg
- 3 tbsp butter, melted

DIRECTIONS

1. In a bowl, mix all the ingredients until they are well combined.
2. Allow the batter to stand for 4 minutes.
3. Preheat the air fryer to 201°C and spray the air fryer-safe pan with cooking spray.

4. Spread the batter on the pan with the desired thickness.
5. Cook each pancake for 3 minutes until all batter is finished.
6. Serve and enjoy.

 Nutrition- Per Serving:
Calories 346kcal, Total Fat: 14g, Carbs: 48g, Proteins 10g

 Variation: The butter can be replaced with cooking oil.

9. Air Fryer Biscuits and Gravy

Preparation Time:
10 minutes

Cooking time:
15 minutes

Serving:
6

INGREDIENTS

Gravy Ingredients:
- 454g ground sausage, browned
- 118ml cream cheese, melted
- 118ml water
- 118ml heavy whipping cream
- ½ tbsp garlic powder
- 1 tbsp xanthan gum
- Salt and black pepper to taste

Biscuit Ingredients:
- 118gCarb Quick
- 57g cubed butter
- ½ tbsp garlic powder
- ½ tbsp salt
- 29g heavy whipping cream
- 59ml water

DIRECTIONS

1. Mix all the gravy ingredients in a bowl until well combined.
2. Transfer the gravy to the air fryer-safe pan.
3. In a separate bowl, mix the Carb Quick with butter.
4. Stir in the garlic, salt, cream, and water to the Carb Quick mixture until a smooth dough is formed.
5. Make small biscuits from the dough and add them to the gravy.
6. Air fry the biscuits at 176ºC for 15 minutes.
7. Serve and enjoy.

 Nutrition- Per Serving:
Calories 690kcal, Total Fat: 60g, Carbs: 40g, Proteins: 29g

 Variation: The Carb Quick can be replaced with homemade biscuit dough.

10. Air Fryer Scrambled Eggs

Preparation Time:
3 minutes

Cooking time:
7 minutes

Serving:
2

INGREDIENTS

- ⅓tbsp unsalted butter, melted
- 2 eggs, beaten
- 2 tbsp milk
- Salt and black pepper to taste
- 29g cheddar cheese

DIRECTIONS

1. Whisk the butter, eggs, milk, salt, and pepper in a bowl.
2. Transfer the mixture to an air fryer-safe pan and cook it at 149°C for 3 minutes.
3. Stir the eggs, then cook them for an additional 2 minutes.
4. Stir the cheese into the eggs, then cook for 2 minutes.
5. Remove the eggs from the pan and serve.

 Nutrition- Per Serving:
Calories 126kcal, Total Fat:5g, Carbs: 1g, Proteins: 9g

 Variation: The preferred cheese can be used.

1. Air Fryer French Fries

Preparation Time:
10 minutes

Cooking Time:
15 minutes

Serving:
2

INGREDIENTS

- Cooking spray
- 1 russet potato, unpeeled
- 1 tbsp olive oil
- Salt and black pepper to taste

DIRECTIONS

1. Preheat the air fryer to 194°C and spray the air fryer basket with cooking spray.
2. Slice the potato lengthwise into 2 ½ cm sticks.
3. Rinse the potato pieces with clean water and then dry them with a paper towel.
4. Add the potato pieces to a bowl.
5. Pour oil over the potato pieces, then sprinkle them with salt and pepper.
6. Toss the potato sticks until well coated.
7. Transfer the potato sticks to an air fryer basket in a single layer.
8. Cook the fries for 15 minutes, turning them halfway during cooking.
9. Serve and enjoy.

 Nutrition-Per Serving: Calories: 214Kcal, Total Fat: 7g, Carbs: 35g, Protein: 4g

 Variation: The desired seasoning can be used.

---

2. Air Fryer Curly Fries

Preparation Time:
10 minutes

Cooking Time:
30 minutes

Serving:
4

INGREDIENTS

- 2 large potatoes
- 1 tablespoon rapeseed oil
- coarse sea salt and black pepper to taste

DIRECTIONS

1. Slice potatoes into spirals using the medium grating attachment on a spiraliser, cutting the circles with scissors after 4 or 5 rotations.
2. Soak potato spirals in a bowl of water for 20 minutes. Drain and rinse well. Pat potatoes dry with a kitchen roll, removing as much moisture as possible.
3. Place potato spirals in a large resealable food bag. Add oil, salt and pepper; toss to coat.
4. Preheat an air fryer to 180 C.
5. Place half of the potato spirals in the fry basket and insert them into the air fryer. Cook until golden, about 5 minutes.
6. Increase temperature to 200 C. Pull out the fry basket and toss curly fries using tongs. Return basket to the air fryer and continue cooking, occasionally tossing, until golden brown, 10 to 12 minutes.
7. Reduce temperature to 180 C and repeat with remaining potato spirals.

3. Air Fryer Pickles

Preparation Time:
10 minutes

Cooking Time:
16 minutes

Serving:
4

INGREDIENTS

- 4 dill pickles, sliced lengthwise
- 63g all-purpose flour
- ½ tbsp paprika
- ¼ tbsp garlic powder
- ¼ tbsp black pepper
- ¼ tbsp cayenne pepper
- 1 tbsp salt
- 120ml buttermilk
- 1 egg
- 53g bread crumbs
- 2 tbsp olive oil
- Cooking spray

DIRECTIONS

1. Pat dry the pickles with a paper towel.
2. Mix the flour, paprika, garlic powder, black pepper, cayenne pepper, and ½ tablespoon salt in a bowl.
3. Mix buttermilk, egg, and ¼ cup of the flour mixture in a separate bowl.
4. Mix the breadcrumbs, remaining salt, and oil in a different bowl until combined.
5. Coat the pickles with the flour mixture, dip in the buttermilk mixture, and coat with the bread crumbs mixture.
6. Spread the holes in an air fryer basket in a single layer.

7. Cook the pits at 204ºC for 10 minutes.
8. Spray the pickles with cooking spray and cook them for an additional 6 minutes.
9. Serve and enjoy.

 Nutrition-Per Serving: Calories: 223Kcal, Total Fat: 10g, Carbs: 25g, Protein: 6g

 Variation: Onion powder can be used instead of cayenne pepper.

4. Indian Potato and Peas Samosa

Preparation Time:
10 minutes

Cooking Time:
20 minutes

Serving:
20 Samosa's

INGREDIENTS

- 2 tsp oil
- 2 tsp cumin seeds
- 1 1/2 Cup green peas boiled
- 150 boiled potatoes roughly mashed
- 1/2 tsp Turmeric

- 1/2 tsp Chilli Powder
- 1 tsp **Garam masala**
- **Salt to taste**
- **2 Tbsp Coriander leaves**
- 20 Samosa Patty

DIRECTIONS

1. Defrost the Samosa Patty or let it defrost outdoors for at least 30 minutes in advance. I set them aside as soon as I put the potatoes to boil.
2. Heat the oil in a pan, add the cumin seeds and let them crackle. Add the boiled peas, turmeric powder, salt, chilli powder, and garam masala. Mix well. Add the diced or coarsely mashed potatoes to the mixture and mix again. If necessary, sprinkle one teaspoon of water. Sprinkle with coriander leaves, remove the mixture from heat, and set aside the mixture.
3. Carefully remove the pie from the bundle and lay them straight. Place a small portion of the samosa mixture in the left corner. Seal the samosas by beating them on the other edge and turning them carefully until you get the cone. Wet the edges of the pie and give it a light pressure.
4. Repeat the process for the rest of the cupcakes. Remember to cover the prepared samosas with a damp muslin cloth.
5. Preheat the Airfryer for 5 minutes at 180 ⊠ C. Brush the samosas with oil.
6. Place five samosas in the Airfryer and bake at the same temperature for 18-22 minutes or until golden brown in the middle. Repeat the process for the remaining samosas.

7. Serve hot with coriander chutney or date chutney.
8. Nutrition-Per Serving: Calories: 42kcal Carbs: 7.9g Protein: 1.2g Saturated Fat: 0.1g

5. Air Fryer Pizza Sliders

Preparation Time:
10 minutes

Cooking Time:
12 minutes

Serving:
12

INGREDIENTS

- 1 pack of dinner rolls
- 236ml pizza sauce
- 473g mozzarella cheese, shredded
- ¼ red onion, diced
- 75g mixed coloured bell peppers
- 6 black olives, sliced
- Salt and black pepper to taste
- ¼ tbsp dry oregano leaves
- Fresh parsley

For Garlic Butter:

- 57g unsalted butter, melted
- 1 tbsp dry parsley flakes
- ½ tbsp dry oregano leaves
- ½ tbsp dry Italian seasoning
- ¼ tbsp salt
- 3 tbsp parmesan cheese

DIRECTIONS

1. Preheat the air fryer to 188°C.
2. Mix all the garlic butter ingredients in a bowl until well combined, then set aside.
3. Cut the dinner rolls lengthwise into halves.
4. Place one of the halves of the dinner rolls on a flat surface.
5. Spread butter on the dinner roll, the pizza sauce, and the ½ mozzarella cheese.
6. Repeat the process for 11 dinner rolls.
7. Divide the onions, bell peppers, olives, salt, black pepper, oregano, and remaining cheese into all the dinner rolls
8. Cook the dinner rolls for 7 minutes.
9. Spread the butter on the remaining dinner rolls, then place them over the cheese.
10. Brush the dinner rolls with garlic butter and cook them for 5 minutes.
11. Brush the dinner rolls with more garlic butter and sprinkle parsley, then serve.

 Nutrition-Per Serving: Calories: 80Kcal, Total Fat: 4g, Carbs: 5g, Protein: 7g

Variation: Marinara sauce can be used in place of pizza sauce

6. Air Fryer Pizza Margherita

Preparation Time: 5 minutes

Cooking Time: 7 minutes

Serving: 1 Pizza

INGREDIENTS

- Buffalo mozzarella
- Pizza dough 30cm dough will make two personal-sized pizzas
- Olive oil
- Tomato sauce
- Optional toppings to finish: fresh basil, parmesan cheese, pepper flakes

DIRECTION

1. Preheat the air fryer to 190°C. Spray the air fryer basket well with oil. Dry the mozzarella from its liquid well. (To see that the dough gets wet)
2. Roll out pizza dough to the size of your air fryer basket. Carefully transfer it to the air fryer, then brush lightly with a teaspoon or so of olive oil. Spoon on a light layer of tomato sauce and sprinkle with chunks of buffalo mozzarella.
3. For about 7 minutes, until crust is crispy and cheese has melted. Optionally top with basil, grated parmesan, and pepper flakes just before serving.

7. Air Fryer Ravioli

Preparation Time: 5 minutes

Cooking Time: 6 minutes

Serving: 6

INGREDIENTS

- 12 ravioli, frozen
- 121g buttermilk
- 53g breadcrumbs
- Cooking spray

DIRECTIONS

1. Preheat the air fryer to 204°C.
2. Place buttermilk and breadcrumbs in 2 different bowls.

3. Dip each ravioli into buttermilk, then coat with breadcrumbs.
4. Arrange the breaded ravioli in the air fryer in a single layer.
5. Air fry the ravioli for 6 minutes, spraying them with cooking spray halfway during cooking.
6. Serve while hot.

 Nutrition-Per Serving: Calories: 480Kcal, Total Fat: 20g, Carbs: 57g, Protein: 20g

 Variation: the buttermilk can be replaced with eggs.

8. Air Fryer Zucchini Chips

Preparation Time:
10 minutes

Cooking Time:
8 minutes

Serving:
4

INGREDIENTS

- 1 zucchini
- 53g breadcrumbs
- ½ tbsp garlic powder
- ¼ tbsp onion powder
- 1 egg
- 3 tbsp all-purpose flour

DIRECTIONS

1. Slice the zucchini into 2½ cm slices.
2. Mix the breadcrumbs, garlic powder, and onion powder in a bowl.
3. Place the egg and flour in separate bowls.
4. Coat the zucchini in flour, dip it into the egg, and coat them with the breadcrumbs.
5. Air fry the zucchini at 193°C for 8 minutes, flipping them halfway during cooking.
6. Serve and enjoy.

 Nutrition-Per Serving: Calories: 102Kcal, Total Fat: 2g, Carbs: 15g, Protein: 5g

 Variation: different seasons can be used depending on your preference.

9. Air Fryer Sweet Potato Fries

Preparation Time:
4 minutes

Cooking Time:
20 minutes

Serving:
2

INGREDIENTS

- 473g sweet potato
- ½ tbsp salt
- ¼ tbsp black pepper
- ¼ tbsp paprika
- 2 tbsp avocado oil

DIRECTIONS

1. Preheat the air fryer to 193°C.
2. Wash the sweet potato with clean water, then slice them into 2 ½ cm sticks.
3. Dry the sweet potato with a paper towel.
4. Toss the sweet potato pieces, salt, pepper, paprika, and oil in a bowl.
5. Transfer the sweet potato into the air fryer basket and cook them for 20 minutes. Shake the basket halfway during cooking.
6. Serve and enjoy.

 Nutrition-Per Serving: Calories: 236Kcal, Total Fat: 5g, Carbs: 45g, Protein: 4g

 Variation: Coconut oil spray can be used instead of avocado oil.

10. Air Fryer Chicken Wings

Preparation Time:
10 minutes

Cooking Time:
15 minutes

Serving:
2

INGREDIENTS

- 680g chicken wings
- 2 tbsp olive oil
- 1 tbsp smoked paprika
- 1 tbsp chilli powder
- 1 ½ tbsp ground cumin
- 1 ½ tbsp onion powder
- 1 ½ tbsp garlic powder
- 1 ½ tbsp ground black pepper
- 1 ½ tbsp salt
- 1 tbsp cayenne pepper

DIRECTIONS

1. Preheat the air fryer to 190°C.
2. Rinse the chicken with clean water, then dry it with a paper towel.
3. Pour oil over the chicken wings and rub to coat.
4. Mix the paprika, chilli powder, cumin, onion powder, garlic powder, black pepper, salt, and cayenne until well combined.
5. Add the chicken to the seasoning mixture and toss to coat.
6. Transfer the chicken wings to the air fryer.
7. Cook the chicken wings for 15 minutes, flipping them halfway during cooking.
8. Serve while warm.

 Nutrition-Per Serving: Calories: 335Kcal, Total Fat: 23g, Carbs: 9g, Protein: 25g

 Variation: seasonings can be used depending on your preference.

11. Air Fryer Chickpeas

Preparation Time:
5 minutes

Cooking Time:
17 minutes

Serving:
3

INGREDIENTS

- 473g can Garbanzo beans, drained
- Avocado cooking spray
- Chilli lime seasoning

DIRECTIONS

1. Preheat the air fryer to 198°C.
2. Place the chickpeas in the air fryer and cook them for about 5 minutes.
3. Open the basket, spray the chickpeas with cooking spray, and shake to coat.
4. Cook the chickpeas for 10 minutes, shaking the basket halfway during cooking.
5. Open the basket and add the seasoning and shake to combine.
6. Cook the chickpeas for another 2 minutes.
7. Serve and enjoy.

 Nutrition-Per Serving: Calories: 380Kcal, Total Fat: 27g, Carbs: 3g, Protein: 34g

 Variation: ranch seasoning can be used instead of chilli lime seasoning.

1. Air Fryer Roasted Asparagus and Potatoes

Preparation Time:
10 minutes

Cooking Time:
5 minutes

Serving:
4

INGREDIENTS

- 4 young potatoes cut into small pieces
- 454g asparagus, cut into small pieces
- 2 stalks scallions, chopped
- 4 tbsp olive oil
- 1 tbsp dried dill
- 1 tbsp salt
- ½ tbsp black pepper

DIRECTIONS

1. Place the potatoes in a saucepan, then cover them with water.
2. Bring the potatoes to a simmer until tender.
3. Drain the potatoes, then set them aside.
4. In a bowl, toss asparagus, scallions, and two tablespoons of olive oil.
5. Transfer the asparagus to an air fryer and cook for 5 minutes at 176ºC.
6. Mix the potatoes, roasted asparagus and scallions, remaining oil, dill, salt, and pepper in a bowl.
7. Serve and enjoy.

 Nutrition-Per Serving: Calories: 449Kcal, Total Fat: 14g, Carbs: 73g, Protein: 12g

 Variation: The desired spices can be used.

---

2. Buttermilk Air Fried Mushrooms

Preparation Time:
30 minutes

Cooking Time:
15 minutes

Serving:
2

INGREDIENTS

- Cooking spray
- 250g oyster mushroom
- 240ml buttermilk
- 188g all-purpose flour
- 1 tbsp salt
- 1 tbsp black pepper
- 1 tbsp garlic powder
- 1 tbsp onion powder
- 1 tbsp smoked paprika
- 1 tbsp cumin
- 1 tbsp olive oil

DIRECTIONS

1. Preheat the air fryer to 190ºC and spray the air fryer-safe pan with cooking spray.
2. In a bowl, toss the mushroom and buttermilk. Allow the mixture to stand for 15 minutes.
3. Mix the flour, salt, pepper, garlic powder, onion powder, paprika, and cumin in a separate bowl until well combined.
4. Coat the mushroom with the flour mixture, dip in the buttermilk, and coat with the flour mixture.
5. Arrange the mushroom on the pan in a single layer, leaving space between each mushroom.
6. Air fry the mushrooms for 5 minutes.
7. Brush the mushrooms with oil, then cook for 10 minutes.
8. Serve and enjoy.

 Nutrition-Per Serving: Calories: 356Kcal, Total Fat: 10g, Carbs: 58g, Protein: 12g

 Variation: the spices can be adjusted to fit your preference.

3. Air Fryer Baked Potatoes

Preparation Time:
10 minutes

Cooking Time:
45 minutes

Serving:
4

INGREDIENTS

- 4 potatoes
- 2 tbsp olive oil
- Salt to taste
- Black pepper to taste
- Garlic powder to taste
- Fresh parsley
- 4 tbsp butter

DIRECTIONS

1. Add the potatoes and olive oil into a bowl and toss to coat.
2. Season the potatoes with salt, black pepper, garlic powder, and fresh parsley.
3. Transfer the potatoes to the air fryer and cook at 203°C for 45 minutes.
4. Cut a slice of the potatoes and force the potato's flesh up.
5. Place 1 tablespoon of butter over each potato.
6. Serve and enjoy.

 Nutrition-Per Serving: Calories: 410Kcal, Total Fat: 14g, Carbs: 66g, Protein: 8g

 Variation: Cajun spices can be used for the seasoning.

4. Air Fryer Stuffed Baby Artichokes

Preparation Time:
20 minutes

Cooking Time:
15 minutes

Serving:
10

INGREDIENTS

- 907g baby artichokes
- 946ml of water
- 59ml lemon juice
- 225g cream cheese
- 22½g spinach, frozen
- 8 garlic cloves, minced
- 2 tbsp olive oil
- ½ tbsp sea salt
- ¼ tbsp black pepper
- 50g parmesan cheese, grated

DIRECTIONS

1. Cut the artichoke stems leaving ½ cm long.
2. Remove the artichoke's outer petals, then cut them into halves.
3. In a bowl, mix water and lemon juice.
4. Place the artichokes in the lime water with the cut side down, then set aside.
5. In a bowl, mash the cream cheese, spinach, and garlic.
6. Take the artichokes out of the lime water and dry them with a paper towel.
7. Toss the artichoke, oil, salt, and pepper in a bowl until well coated.
8. Spread the spinach mixture over each artichoke, then sprinkle them with parmesan.
9. Arrange the artichokes in an air fryer and cook them at 203°C for 15 minutes.

10. Serve and enjoy.

 Nutrition-Per Serving:
Calories: 176Kcal, Total Fat: 12g, Carbs: 13g, Protein: 7g

 Variation: Cream cheese can be used in place of parmesan cheese.

5. Air Fryer Buffalo Cauliflower

Preparation Time:
10 minutes

Cooking Time:
12 minutes

Serving:
3

INGREDIENTS

- 5.7kg cauliflower head, cut into florets
- 118ml cayenne pepper sauce
- 2 tbsp butter, melted
- 2 tbsp vinegar
- ⅛ tbsp garlic powder
- Salad dressing

DIRECTIONS

1. Preheat the air fryer to 204ºC.
2. Mix the cauliflower, cayenne pepper sauce, butter, vinegar, and garlic powder in a bowl until well combined.
3. Transfer the cauliflower to the air fryer basket and cook for 12 minutes. Shake the basket halfway during the cooking.
4. Serve the cauliflower with salad dressing.

 Nutrition-Per Serving: Calories: 228Kcal, Total Fat: 20g, Carbs: 11g, Protein: 4g

 Variation: Blue cheese dip can be used instead of salad dressing.

6. Air Fryer Carrot Fries

Preparation Time:
5 minutes

Cooking Time:
20 minutes

Serving:
4

INGREDIENTS

- 4 carrots, peeled and sliced lengthwise
- 1 tbsp cornflour
- 1 tbsp paprika
- ½ tbsp garlic powder
- 1 tbsp olive oil
- Salt to taste

DIRECTIONS

1. Preheat the air fryer to 189°C.
2. Mix carrots, cornflour, paprika, garlic powder, and olive oil in a bowl.
3. Transfer the seasoned carrots to the air fryer basket and spread them in a single layer without overlapping.
4. Cook the carrots for 20 minutes, flipping them halfway during cooking.
5. Transfer the carrot fries to a serving platter and sprinkle them with salt.
6. Serve and enjoy.

Nutrition-Per Serving:
Calories: 30Kcal, Total Fat: 1g, Carbs: 5g, Protein: 1g

Variation:
Corn starch can be used in place of corn flour.

---

7. Air Fryer Cauliflower Chickpea Tacos

Preparation Time:
10 minutes

Cooking Time:
20 minutes

Serving:
4

INGREDIENTS

- 256g cauliflower florets
- 404g can of chickpeas, drained and rinsed
- 2 tbsp olive oil
- 2 tbsp taco seasoning
- 8 corn tortilla
- 2 avocado sliced
- 280g cabbage, shredded
- Coconut yoghurt

DIRECTIONS

1. Preheat the air fryer to 198°C.
2. Toss the cauliflower, chickpeas, olive oil, and taco seasoning in a bowl.
3. Transfer the cauliflower mixture to the air fryer basket and cook for 20 minutes. Shake the basket occasionally during the cooking.
4. Serve the cauliflower and chickpeas in tacos with avocado slices, cabbage, and coconut yoghurt.

Nutrition-Per Serving: Calories: 507Kcal, Total Fat: 15g, Carbs: 76g, Protein: 20g

 Variation: Coconut yoghurt can be replaced with regular yoghurt.

8. Air Fryer Brussels Sprouts

Preparation Time:
10 minutes

Cooking Time:
10 minutes

Serving:
4

INGREDIENTS

- 454g brussels sprouts, trimmed
- 2 tbsp olive oil
- ¼ tbsp salt
- ¼ tbsp garlic powder

DIRECTIONS

1. Add all the ingredients into a bowl and toss to coat.
2. Transfer the Brussels to an air fryer basket and cook them at 187ºC for about 8 minutes. Shake the basket halfway during the cooking.
3. Plate the Brussels and serve.

 Nutrition-Per Serving: Calories: 110Kcal, Total Fat: 7g, Carbs: 11g, Protein: 4g

Variation: Favorite seasonings can be used.

9. Air Fryer Kale and Potato Nuggets

Preparation Time:
10 minutes

Cooking Time:
47 minutes

Serving:
4

INGREDIENTS

- 364g potatoes, finely chopped
- 1 tbsp extra virgin oil
- 1 garlic clove, minced
- 30ml almond milk
- ¼ tbsp salt
- ⅛ tbsp black pepper
- 268g kale, coarsely chopped
- Vegetable oil spray

DIRECTIONS

1. Add the potatoes and water to a saucepan and then boil them.
2. Cook the potatoes for 30 minutes until they are tender.
3. Drain the potatoes and set them aside.
4. Pour oil into a skillet and heat it over medium heat.
5. Sauté garlic for 3 minutes.
6. Add the potatoes, garlic, almond milk, salt, and pepper to a bowl and mash using a potato masher.
7. Stir in kale to the mashed potatoes.
8. Preheat the air fryer to 198°C and spray the air fryer basket with oil spray.
9. Make 2 ½ cm nuggets with the potato-kale mixture.
10. Air fry the nuggets for 14 minutes, shaking the basket after 6 minutes.
11. Serve and enjoy.

 Nutrition-Per Serving: Calories: 380Kcal, Total Fat: 27g, Carbs: 3g, Protein: 34g

 Variation: canola oil can be used in place of extra virgin oil **Brussels**

1. Air Fryer Avocado Fries

Preparation Time:
5 minutes

Cooking Time:
10 minutes

Serving:
2

INGREDIENTS

- 1 ripe avocado, sliced
- 106g bread crumbs
- ½ tbsp salt
- ½ can chickpea aquafaba

DIRECTIONS

1. Preheat the air fryer to 198°C.
2. In a bowl, mix the breadcrumbs and salt.
3. Pour the aquafaba into a separate bowl.
4. Dip the avocado slice in the aquafaba, then coat it with bread crumbs.
5. Carefully arrange the avocado slices in the air fryer basket in a single layer.
6. Air fry the avocado for 10 minutes.
7. Serve and enjoy.

 Nutrition-Per Serving: Calories: 295Kcal, Total Fat: 17g, Carbs: 31g, Protein: 8g

 Variation: Seasoned cornmeal can be used instead of breadcrumbs.

---

2. Air Fryer Green Beans

Preparation Time:
10 minutes

Cooking Time:
12 minutes

Serving:
4

INGREDIENTS

- 355g fresh green bean beans, trimmed
- 1 tbsp sesame oil
- 1 tbsp soy sauce
- 1 tbsp rice wine vinegar
- 1 garlic clove, minced

- ½ tbsp red pepper flakes

DIRECTIONS

1. Preheat the air fryer to 204ºC.
2. Add all the ingredients to a bowl and toss to mix.
3. Allow the green beans to marinate for about 5 minutes.
4. Transfer the green beans to the air fryer and cook for 12 minutes. Shake the basket halfway during the cooking.
5. Serve and enjoy.

 Nutrition-Per Serving: Calories: 60Kcal, Total Fat: 4g, Carbs: 7g, Protein: 2g

Variation: Olive oil can be used instead of sesame oil.

3. Air Fryer Peach Pies

Preparation Time:
30 minutes

Cooking Time:
56 minutes

Serving:
8

INGREDIENTS

- 284g fresh peaches, peeled and chopped
- 1 tbsp lemon juice
- 3 tbsp granulated sugar
- 1 tbsp vanilla extract
- ¼ tbsp salt
- 1 tbsp cornstarch
- 296g package rolled unbaked pie crust
- Cooking spray

DIRECTIONS

1. Mix the peaches, lemon juice, sugar, vanilla, and salt in a bowl.
2. Allow the peach mixture to stand for 15 minutes.
3. Drain the peaches and reserve one tablespoon of the marinade.
4. Mix the cornstarch, reserved marinade, and peaches in a separate bowl.
5. Make 10cm circles from the pie crust.
6. Place a spoonful of the peach mixture on each circle and fold the dough over the filling.
7. Crimp the edges of the dough to seal.
8. Make three minor cuts on top of the pies, then coat them with cooking spray.
9. Repeat the process for all the pies
10. Air fry the pies in batches at 176ºC for 14 minutes.
11. Serve and enjoy.

Nutrition–Per Serving: Calories: 314Kcal, Total Fat: 15g, Carbs: 43g, Protein: 3g

 Variation: Fresh peaches can be replaced with frozen peaches.

4. Air Fryer Cherry Tomatoes

Preparation Time:
5 minutes

Cooking Time:
5 minutes

Serving:
4

INGREDIENTS

- 454g cherry tomatoes
- 2 tbsp olive oil
- 1 tbsp salt
- ½ tbsp black pepper

DIRECTIONS

1. Add all the ingredients to a bowl and toss to coat.
2. Transfer the tomatoes to an air fryer basket.
3. Air fry the tomatoes for 5 minutes at 149ºC.
4. Serve and enjoy.

 Nutrition–Per Serving: Calories: 133Kcal, Total Fat: 7g, Carbs: 19g, Protein: 1g

Variation: the desired seasonings can be used.

5. Air Fryer Butternut Squash

Preparation Time:
10 minutes

Cooking Time:
20 minutes

Serving:
4

INGREDIENTS

- 4 butternut squash, chopped into cubes
- 2 tbsp extra virgin oil
- 1 tbsp maple syrup
- 1 tbsp dried oregano
- ½ tbsp garlic powder
- ½ tbsp smoked paprika
- ½ tbsp salt

¼ tbsp ground chipotle chilli
pepper

DIRECTIONS

1. Add all the ingredients to a bowl and toss to coat.
2. Arrange the butternut in an air fryer basket in a single layer.
3. Air fry the butternut at 204°C for 20 minutes.
4. Serve while hot.

 Nutrition-Per Serving: Calories: 140Kcal, Total Fat: 7g, Carbs: 21g, Protein: 2g

Variation: Seasoning the butternuts may be done following your preference.

---

6. Salad and Falafels

Preparation Time:
20 minutes

Cooking Time:
15 minutes

Serving:
2

INGREDIENTS

- 425g 1 can **chickpeas, drained and** rinsed
- 64g cilantro
- 32g fresh parsley
- 1/2 small onion
- 3 cloves garlic

- 1 teaspoon cumin
- 1 teaspoon coriander
- 1 teaspoon ground paprika
- 1/4 teaspoon Cayenne pepper, more for a spicier flavour
- 1/2 teaspoon salt

For the Salad:

- 57g lettuce, chopped
- 45g cherry tomatoes, halved
- 1 small cucumber, cut into slices

- 26g red onion, cut into slices
- 25g pitted black olives, slices
- Vegan Tzatziki Sauce

DIRECTIONS

1. Line the air fryer basket with parchment paper, spray with cooking spray or brush with cooking oil.
2. Add chickpeas to the food processor with cilantro, parsley, onion, garlic, cumin, coriander, paprika, cayenne pepper, salt, and pulse.

3. The mixture shouldn't be processed until smooth but still grainy but able to stick together.
4. Scoop out tablespoon sizes of falafel mixture and roll in between the palm of your hands into balls.
5. Place in a single layer on the parchment paper-lined air fryer. Spray with cooking spray.
6. Bake at 176⁰C for 15 minutes, turning halfway.
7. Repeat until all the mixture is used up.

7. Air Fryer Cauliflower Bites

Preparation Time:
2 hrs 5 minutes

Cooking Time:
12 minutes

Serving:
4

INGREDIENTS

- 207g cauliflower, minced
- 104g sweet potato, grated
- 74g carrot, grated
- 89g parsnips, chopped
- 2 tbsp garlic puree
- 1 tbsp chives
- 1 tbsp paprika
- 1 tbsp mixed spice
- 2 tbsp oregano
- Salt and black pepper to taste
- 45g desiccated coconut
- 102g gluten-free oats
- Cooking spray

DIRECTIONS

1. Mix cauliflower, sweet potato, carrot, and parsnips until well combined.
2. Add garlic, chives, paprika, mixed spice, oregano, salt, and pepper to the vegetable mixture.
3. Make medium-sized balls from the vegetable mixture.
4. Refrigerate the veggie balls for 2 hours.
5. Blend the coconut and oats in a blender, then transfer the flour to a bowl.
6. Coat the veggie balls with the flour mixture, then place them on an air fryer-safe pan.
7. Spritz the veggie balls with cooking spray.
8. Cook the veggies at 204ºC for 12 minutes, rolling the ball after 10 minutes of cooking.
9. Serve and enjoy.

 Nutrition-Per Serving: Calories: 213Kcal, Total Fat: 9g, Carbs: 30g, Protein: 6g

 Variation: Favorite vegetables can be used.

8. Air Fryer Tofu with Broccoli and Carrot

Preparation Time:
10 minutes

Cooking Time:
15 minutes

Serving:
4

INGREDIENTS

For the Tofu:
- 414g extra-firm tofu
- 1 tbsp sesame oil
- 1 tbsp soy sauce

For the Stirfry:
- 2 sliced carrots
- 1 broccoli, chopped
- 1 tbsp sesame oil

For the Sauce:
- 2 tbsp orange zest
- 118ml orange juice
- 3 tbsp rice vinegar
- 2 tbsp soy sauce
- 2 tbsp sugar
- 2 tbsp cornstarch
- ¼ tbsp salt
- 2 minced garlic cloves

DIRECTIONS

1. Preheat the air fryer to 198°C.
2. Add the tofu, sesame oil, and soy sauce to a bowl and toss to mix.
3. Place the tofu in the air fryer basket and cook for 5 minutes.
4. Meanwhile, in a bowl, combine the carrots, broccoli, and oil.
5. Stir in the carrots and broccoli to the air fryer and cook for about 2 minutes.
6. Mix all the sauce ingredients until all cornstarch dissolves.
7. Pour the sauce into the skillet and cook until the sauce thickens.
8. Add the tofu and veggies to the skillet and mix.
9. Plate the tofu, stir fry, and serve.

 Nutrition–Per Serving: Calories: 298Kcal, Total Fat: 13g, Carbs: 32g, Protein: 16g

 Variation: preferred vegetables may be used.

---

9. Air Fryer Spicy Cauliflower Stir-Fry

Preparation Time:
5 minutes

Cooking Time:
30 minute

Serving:
4

INGREDIENTS

- 1 cauliflower, cut into florets
- 2 tbsp olive oil
- 2 ½ onions, thinly sliced
- 5 garlic cloves, sliced
- 1 ½ tbsp tamari
- 1 tbsp rice vinegar
- ½ tbsp coconut sugar
- 1 tbsp sriracha
- Salt and pepper to taste
- 2 scallions

DIRECTIONS

1. Preheat the air fryer to 177ºC.
2. Add the cauliflower and oil to a bowl and toss to coat.
3. Place the cauliflower in the air fryer basket and cook for 10 minutes.
4. Stir in the onions to the cauliflower and cook for 10 minutes.
5. Stir in garlic to the cauliflower and cook for 5 minutes.
6. Meanwhile, mix tamari, rice vinegar, coconut sugar, sriracha, salt, and pepper in a bowl.
7. Stir the sauce mixture into the cauliflower and cook for 5 minutes.
8. Plate the cauliflower and garnish with the scallions.
9. Serve and enjoy.

 Nutrition–Per Serving: Calories: 93Kcal, Total Fat: 3g, Carbs: 13g, Protein: 3g

Variation: Favorite hot sauce can be used in place of sriracha.

10. Air Fryer Vegan Burger

Preparation Time:
5 minutes

Cooking Time:
10 minute

Serving:
4

INGREDIENTS

- 400g white beans rinsed and drained (I used cannellini beans)
- 65g oats
- 15g fresh cilantro finely chopped
- 1/2 small onion grated or very finely diced
- 1/2 bell pepper, deseeded preferably grated or very finely diced
- juice of 1 lemon
- 3 Tablespoon sriracha sauce or tomato sauce
- 1 1/2 teaspoon Italian seasoning or oregano
- 1 teaspoon ground cumin
- 1/2 teaspoon smoked paprika
- 1/2 teaspoon garlic powder
- sea salt to taste

DIRECTIONS

1. Mash the beans in a mixing bowl.
2. Add in oats, cilantro, onion, bell pepper, lemon juice, sriracha sauce (or tomato sauce), herbs and spices and mix.
3. Divide and shape into four patties.
4. Preheat Air Fryer to 180C. Place patties in the basket, spray with olive oil or cooking spray and cook for 9-10 minutes, flipping halfway through.
5. Create burgers with buns, patties and then desired toppings.

 Nutrition: Calories: 182kcal, Carbs: 34g, Protein: 10g, Fat: 1g

1. Air Fryer Scallops

Preparation Time: 10 minutes	**Cooking Time:** 8 minutes	**Serving:** 2

INGREDIENTS

- 55g mashed potato flakes
- 32g bread crumbs, seasoned
- ⅛ tbsp salt
- ⅛ tbsp black pepper
- 6 scallops
- 2 tbsp all-purpose flour
- 1 egg, beaten
- Flavoured cooking spray.

DIRECTIONS

1. Preheat the air fryer to 204ºC.
2. Mix the potato flakes, bread crumbs, salt, and pepper in a bowl.
3. In a separate bowl, toss the scallops with flour.
4. Place the egg on a shallow plate.
5. Dip the scallops in the egg, then coat them with the potato mixture.
6. Place the scallops in the air fryer basket and spritz them with cooking spray.
7. Cook the scallops for 8 minutes, turning them halfway during the cooking.
8. Serve and enjoy.

 Nutrition-Per Serving: Calories: 298Kcal, Total Fat: 5g, Carbs: 32g, Protein: 27g

 Variation: Favorite seafood seasoning may be used.

---

2. Air Fryer Pretzel Crusted Catfish

Preparation Time:
10 minutes

Cooking Time:
12 minutes

Serving:
2

INGREDIENTS

- 4 catfish fillets
- ½ tbsp salt
- ½ tbsp black pepper
- 2 eggs
- 5 1/3 tbsp dijon mustard

- 2 tbsp 2% milk
- 63g all-purpose flour
- 946ml honey mustard miniature pretzel, crushed
- Cooking spray

DIRECTIONS

1. Preheat the air fryer to 162°C.
2. Season the catfish with salt and pepper.
3. In a bowl, whisk the eggs, Dijon mustard, and milk.
4. Place the flour and pretzels in different bowls.
5. Coat the catfish with flour, dip them into the egg mixture, and coat them with pretzels.
6. Arrange the catfish in the air fryer basket, then spray them with cooking spray.
7. Cook the catfish for 12 minutes.
8. Serve and enjoy.

 Nutrition-Per Serving: Calories: 466Kcal, Total Fat: 14g, Carbs: 44g, Protein: 34g

 Variation: Yogurt can be used in place of 2% milk.

3. Air Fryer Coconut Shrimp and Apricot Sauce

Preparation Time:
25 minutes

Cooking Time:
8 minutes

Serving:
6

INGREDIENTS

- Cooking spray

- 454g shrimp, uncooked

- 83g sweetened coconut, shredded
- 106g bread crumbs
- 4 egg whites
- 3 dashes of hot sauce
- ¼ tbsp salt
- ¼ tbsp black pepper
- 63g all-purpose flour

For the Sauce:
- 320g apricot preserves
- 1 tbsp cider vinegar
- ¼ tbsp red pepper flakes, crushed

DIRECTIONS

1. Preheat the air fryer to 190ºC and grease the air fryer-safe pan with cooking spray.
2. Peel and devein the shrimp.
3. In a bowl, mix the coconut and the breadcrumbs.
4. Whisk the eggs, hot sauce, salt, and pepper in a separate bowl.
5. Place the flour in a different bowl.
6. Coat the shrimp with flour, then dip in the egg and finally coat with the coconut mixture.
7. Arrange the shrimps on the air fryer pan.
8. Cook the shrimp for 8 minutes, turning them halfway during the cooking.
9. Meanwhile, prepare a sauce by mixing all the sauce ingredients in a saucepan.
10. Cook the sauce over medium heat, occasionally stirring, until all the preserves melt.
11. Plate the shrimp and serve with the sauce.

 Nutrition-Per Serving: Calories: 410Kcal, Total Fat: 10g, Carbs: 57g, Protein: 24g

 Variation: Favourite sauce can be prepared.

4. Air Fryer Crab patties

Preparation Time: 20 minutes

Cooking Time: 10 minutes

Serving: 2

INGREDIENTS

- 1 sweet red pepper, chopped
- 1 celery rib, chopped
- 3 green onions, chopped
- 2 egg whites

- 3 tbsp reduced-fat mayonnaise
- ¼ tbsp horseradish
- ¼ tbsp salt

- 106g bread crumbs
- 135g lump crabmeat
- Cooking spray

For the Sauce:

- 1 celery rib, chopped
- 71g reduced-fat mayonnaise
- 1 green onion, chopped

- 1 tbsp sweet pickle relish
- ½ tbsp horseradish
- ¼ tbsp salt

DIRECTIONS

1. Preheat the air fryer to 190°C.
2. Mix the pepper, celery, onions, egg whites, mayonnaise, horseradish, and salt in a bowl.
3. Stir in the crab meat until well combined.
4. Place the breadcrumbs in a separate bowl.
5. Scoop 2 spoonfuls of the crab mixture and make patties.
6. Coat the patties with the breadcrumbs and place them in the air fryer basket.
7. Spritz the crab patties with cooking spray.
8. Cook the patties for 12 minutes, flipping them halfway during the cooking.
9. Meanwhile, make a sauce by processing all the sauce ingredients in a food processor.
10. Serve the patties with sauce.

 Nutrition-Per Serving: Calories: 49Kcal, Total Fat: 2g, Carbs: 3g, Protein: 3g

Variation: Favorite sauce can be prepared.

---

5. Air Fryer Shrimp Tacos with Cabbage Slaw

Preparation Time:
5 minutes

Cooking Time:
10 minutes

Serving:
4

INGREDIENTS

- 200g coleslaw mix
- 4g fresh cilantro minced
- 2 tbsp lime juice
- 2 tbsp honey
- ¼ tbsp salt
- 1 jalapeno pepper, deceased and minced
- 2 eggs

- 118ml milk
- 53g bread crumbs
- 1 tbsp cumin
- 1 tbsp garlic powder
- 63g all-purpose flour
- Cooking spray
- 1 avocado slices

DIRECTIONS

1. Add the coleslaw mix, cilantro, lime juice, honey, salt, and jalapeno, then toss to coat. Set aside.
2. Preheat the air fryer to 190ºC
3. In another bowl, whisk the eggs and milk.
4. Mix the breadcrumbs, cumin, and garlic powder in a separate bowl.
5. Place the flour in a different bowl.
6. Coat the shrimp with flour, dip them in the egg mixture, and then coat them with bread crumbs.
7. Arrange the shrimps in the air fryer basket in a single layer.
8. Spray the shrimps with cooking spray and cook them for 3 minutes.
9. Turn the shrimp and spray them with cooking spray.
10. Cook the shrimp for an additional 3 minutes.
11. Serve the shrimp in tortillas with avocado and coleslaw mix.

 Nutrition-Per Serving: Calories: 380Kcal, Total Fat: 27g, Carbs: 3g, Protein: 34g

 Variation: cooking spray can be replaced by cooking oil.

6. Air Fryer Whole Sea Bream

Preparation Time:
10 minutes

Cooking Time:
16 minutes

Serving:
4

INGREDIENTS

- 31g all-purpose flour
- 2 tbsp old bay seasoning
- 5 garlic cloves, minced
- Pinch of salt
- 1 whole sea bream
- Cooking spray

DIRECTIONS

1. In a bowl, mix the flour with old bay seasoning.
2. In a separate bowl, combine the garlic and salt.
3. Make several cuts on both sides of the sea bream.
4. Rub the sea bream with the garlic paste, then coat it with the seasoned flour.
5. Place the fish in an air fryer tray and spritz with cooking spray.
6. Air fry the fish at 198ºC for 16 minutes flipping it halfway through cooking.
7. Serve and enjoy.

Nutrition-Per Serving: Calories: 658Kcal, Total Fat: 23g, Carbs: 8g, Protein: 105g

 Variation: Seasoning may be done as desired.

7. Air Fryer Spicy Bay Scallops

Preparation Time:
5 minutes

Cooking Time:
10 minutes

Serving:
4

INGREDIENTS

- 454g bay scallops, dried
- 2 tbsp smoked paprika
- 2 tbsp chilli powder
- 2 tbsp olive oil
- 1 tbsp garlic powder
- ¼ tbsp ground black pepper
- ⅛ tbsp cayenne red pepper

DIRECTIONS

1. Preheat the air fryer to 204°C.
2. In a bowl, mix all the ingredients until well combined.
3. Transfer the scallops to an air fryer basket.
4. Cook the scallops for 8 minutes, shaking the basket halfway during the cooking time.
5. Serve and enjoy.

 Nutrition-Per Serving: Calories: 380Kcal, Total Fat: 27g, Carbs: 3g, Protein: 34g

 Variation: Seasoning of your preference can be used.

8. Air Fryer Old Bay Grilled Shrimp Skewers

Preparation Time:
10 minutes

Cooking Time:
5 minutes

Serving:
8

INGREDIENTS

- 454g shrimp, peeled and deveined
- 8 skewers
- 118ml old bay seasoning

DIRECTIONS

1. Thread the shrimp into the skewers
2. Sprinkle the shrimp with the seasoning.
3. Place the skewed shrimp in the air fryer basket.
4. Air fry the shrimp at 204ºC for 5 minutes.
5. Serve and enjoy.

 Nutrition-Per Serving: Calories: 57Kcal, Total Fat: 1g, Carbs: 0g, Protein: 11g

Variation: Preferred seasoning can be used

---

9. Air Fryer Crumb-Topped Sole

Preparation Time:
10 minutes

Cooking Time:
10 minutes

Serving:
4

INGREDIENTS

- 3 tbsp mayonnaise
- 3 tbsp parmesan cheese, grated
- 2 tbsp mustard seed
- ¼ tbsp black pepper
- 4 sole fillet
- 106g bread crumbs
- 1 finely chopped green onion
- ½ tbsp ground mustard
- 2 tbsp melted butter
- Cooking spray

DIRECTIONS

1. Preheat the air fryer to 190ºC.
2. Mix the mayonnaise, two tablespoons of cheese, mustard seed, and pepper in a bowl.
3. Spread the mayonnaise mixture on both sides of the fillets.
4. Cook the fillets for 3 minutes.
5. Meanwhile, mix bread crumbs, onion, ground mustard, remaining cheese, and butter in a bowl.
6. Gently spread the bread crumbs mixture on the fillets, then mist them with cooking spray.
7. Air fry the fillets for another 3 minutes.
8. Plate the fillets and serve.

 Nutrition-Per Serving: Calories: 233Kcal, Total Fat: 10g, Carbs: 8g, Protein:

24g

 Variation: Greek yoghurt can be used in place of mayonnaise.

10. Air Fryer Salmon with Maple- Dijon Glaze

Preparation Time:
10 minutes

Cooking Time:
6 minutes

Serving:
4

INGREDIENTS

- 3 tbsp butter
- 3 tbsp maple syrup
- 1 tbsp dijon mustard
- 1 lemon juice
- 1 garlic clove, minced
- 4 salmon fillets
- 1 tbsp olive oil
- ¼ tbsp salt
- ¼ tbsp black pepper

DIRECTIONS

1. Preheat the air fryer to 204°C.
2. Melt butter in a saucepan over medium heat.
3. Stir in the butter with maple syrup, Dijon mustard, lemon juice, and garlic.
4. Allow the butter mixture to simmer for 3 minutes until the mixture thickens. Remove from heat and set aside.
5. Brush the salmon with oil and season it with salt and pepper.
6. Place the salmon in the air fryer basket and cook for 6 minutes.
7. Serve the fillet with the prepared sauce.

 Nutrition-Per Serving: Calories: 329Kcal, Total Fat: 24g, Carbs: 11g, Protein: 20g

 Variation: Dijon mustard can be replaced with soy sauce.

1. Air Fryer Chicken and Broccoli

Preparation Time:
10 minutes

Cooking Time:
20 minutes

Serving:
4

INGREDIENTS

- 3 tbsp olive oil
- ½ tbsp garlic powder
- 1 tbsp minced ginger
- 1 tbsp low sodium soy sauce
- 1 tbsp rice vinegar
- 1 tbsp sesame oil
- 2 tbsp hot sauce
- ½ tbsp salt
- Black pepper to taste
- 454g chicken breast, boneless and skinless
- 227g broccoli florets
- 227g onion, sliced

DIRECTIONS

1. Preheat the air fryer to 193ºC
2. Make the marinade by mixing olive oil, garlic powder, ginger, soy sauce, vinegar, sesame oil, hot sauce, salt, and pepper.
3. Place the chicken in a bowl and pour half of the marinade. Stir to coat.
4. Mix the broccoli, onions, and remaining marinade in a separate bowl.
5. Allow the chicken and the broccoli to stand for 5 minutes.
6. Transfer the chicken to an air fryer tray and cook for 10 minutes.
7. Add the broccoli and the marinade to the air fryer.
8. Cook the chicken and broccoli for 10 minutes, stirring them halfway during the cooking.
9. Serve while warm.

 Nutrition-Per Serving: Calories: 224Kcal, Total Fat: 10g, Carbs: 3g, Protein: 26g

 Variation: Apple cider vinegar can be used in place of rice vinegar.

---

2. Air Fryer Turkey Breast

Preparation Time:
5 minutes

Cooking Time:
55 minutes

Serving:
10

INGREDIENTS

- 1.8kg turkey breast, skin in
- 1 tbsp olive oil
- 2 tbsp salt
- ½ tbsp dry turkey seasoning

DIRECTIONS

1. Rub the turkey with oil.
2. Season the turkey with salt and dry turkey seasoning.
3. Preheat the air fryer to 176°C.
4. Place the turkey in the air fryer basket with the skin side down.
5. Cook the turkey for 20 minutes.
6. Turn the turkey and cook for an additional 35 minutes.
7. Allow the turkey to cool for 10 minutes, then serve.

 Nutrition-Per Serving: Calories: 226Kcal, Total Fat: 10g, Carbs: 0g, Protein: 33g

 Variation: Poultry seasoning can be used in place of dry turkey seasoning.

3. Air Fryer Chicken Tenders

Preparation Time:
5 minutes

Cooking Time:
30 minutes

Serving:
4

INGREDIENTS

- 567g chicken tenders
- 2 eggs, beaten
- 1 tbsp salt
- Black pepper to taste
- 53g seasoned breadcrumbs
- Olive oil spray
- Lemon wedges

DIRECTIONS

1. Season the chicken with salt and pepper.
2. Place the egg and breadcrumbs in separate bowls.
3. Dip the chicken in the egg, then coat it with breadcrumbs.
4. Spritz the chicken tenders with olive oil spray.
5. Preheat the air fryer to 204g°C.
6. Cook the chicken in batches for 6 minutes on each side.
7. Serve the chicken tenders with lemon wedges.

 Nutrition-Per Serving: Calories: 291Kcal, Total Fat: 7g, Carbs: 17g, Protein: 39g

 Variation: Almond flour can be used in place of breadcrumbs.

4. Air Fryer Chicken Drumsticks

Preparation Time:
5 minutes

Cooking Time:
20 minutes

Serving:
4

INGREDIENTS

- 1 tbsp sea salt
- 1 tbsp fresh cracked pepper
- 1 tbsp garlic powder
- 1 tbsp paprika
- ½ tbsp cumin
- 8 chicken drumsticks
- 2 tbsp olive oil

DIRECTIONS

1. Mix salt, pepper, garlic powder, paprika, and cumin in a bowl.
2. Add the chicken and oil to a separate bowl and toss to coat.
3. Sprinkle the seasoning over the chicken.
4. Preheat the air fryer to 204°C.
5. Transfer the drumsticks to an air fryer basket.
6. Cook the drumsticks for 20 minutes, flipping them halfway through cooking.
7. Serve while hot.

 Nutrition-Per Serving: Calories: 200Kcal, Total Fat: 12g, Carbs: 1g, Protein: 23g

 Variation: Favorite seasonings can be used.

5. Air Fryer Turkey cutlets

Preparation Time: 10 minutes | **Cooking Time:** 10 minutes | **Serving:** 2

INGREDIENTS

- 2 turkey cutlets
- 1 tbsp butter
- Salt and black pepper to taste
- Parsley

For the Mushroom Sauce:

- 1 can of cream of mushroom soup
- 118ml milk
- Pinch of pepper

DIRECTIONS

1. Preheat the air fryer to 193°C.
2. Spread the butter on the turkey cutlets, then sprinkle them with salt and pepper.
3. Place the turkey cutlets in an air fryer basket and cook for 10 minutes.
4. Meanwhile, prepare the mushroom sauce by mixing the sauce ingredients in a saucepan.
5. Cook the sauce over medium heat for 8 minutes, stirring occasionally.
6. Plate the turkey cutlets.
7. Serve cutlets with mushroom sauce and sprinkled parsley.

 Nutrition-Per Serving: Calories: 380Kcal, Total Fat: 27g, Carbs: 3g, Protein: 34g

 Variation: Mushroom sauce can be swapped out with favourite gravy

6. Air Fryer Cheddar Ranch Chicken Tenders

Preparation Time: 10 minutes | **Cooking Time:** 25 minutes | **Serving:** 8

INGREDIENTS

- Cooking spray
- 2 tbsp all-purpose flour
- 2 tbsp Montreal chicken seasoning
- 71g bread crumbs
- 117g sharp cheddar cheese
- 79g ranch dressing
- 189g chicken tenders, boneless and skinless

DIRECTIONS

1. Line the air fryer basket with parchment paper, then spray it with cooking spray.
2. In a bowl, mix the flour and chicken seasoning.
3. In another bowl, mix the bread crumbs and cheese.
4. Place the ranch dressing in a different bowl.
5. Coat the chicken with flour mixture, dip it into ranch dressing, and coat them with the bread crumb mixture.
6. Preheat the air fryer to 162°C.
7. Transfer the chicken to the air fryer basket and cook for 10 minutes.
8. Turn the chicken, then cook for an additional 15 minutes.
9. Serve and enjoy.

 Nutrition-Per Serving: Calories: 150Kcal, Total Fat: 7g, Carbs: 8g, Protein: 13g

 Variation: Ranch dressing can be replaced with mayonnaise.

7. Air Fryer Parmesan Crusted Chicken

Preparation Time:
5 minutes

Cooking Time:
15 minutes

Serving:
4

INGREDIENTS

- 2 chicken breast
- 112g shredded parmesan
- 106g bread crumbs
- 215g mayonnaise
- 1 tbsp garlic powder
- Parsley for garnishing

DIRECTIONS

1. Cut the chicken breast into halves and pound it with a meat hammer.
2. Sprinkle the chicken with salt.
3. Spread the mayonnaise on both sides of the chicken breasts.
4. Mix the bread crumbs, parmesan, and garlic powder in a bowl.
5. Coat the chicken with the bread crumbs mixture, then transfer them to the air fryer basket.
6. Air fry the chicken at 198°C for 15 minutes, turning them after 10 minutes.
7. Sprinkle some parsley and serve.

 Nutrition-Per Serving: Calories: 663Kcal, Total Fat: 50g, Carbs: 20g, Protein: 31g

 Variation: Bread crumbs can be swapped out with an almond meal.

8. Air Fryer Chicken Kebab

Preparation Time:
1 hr

Cooking Time:
15 minutes

Serving:
4

INGREDIENTS

- 59ml full-fat Greek yoghurt
- 1 tbsp minced garlic
- 1 tbsp tomato paste
- 1 tbsp vegetable oil
- 1 tbsp lemon juice
- 1 tbsp salt
- 1 tbsp ground cumin
- 1 tbsp smoked paprika
- ½ tbsp ground cinnamon
- ½ tbsp black pepper
- ½ tbsp cayenne pepper
- 454g chicken thighs, boneless and skinless
- 4 skewers

DIRECTIONS

1. In a bowl, mix all the ingredients except the chicken until they are well combined.
2. Cut the chicken into 2 ½ cm pieces.
3. Add the chicken pieces to the marinade and mix.
4. Let the chicken marinate for 30 minutes.
5. Place the chicken in the air fryer basket.
6. Set the air fryer to preheat at 187ºC.
7. Cook the chicken for 15 minutes, flipping them after 10 minutes.
8. Add the chicken pieces onto the skewers.
9. Serve and enjoy.

 Nutrition-Per Serving: Calories: 298Kcal, Total Fat: 23g, Carbs: 3g, Protein: 20g

 Variation: Sour cream can be used in place of Greek yoghurt.

---

9. Air Fryer Chicken Nuggets

Preparation Time:
15 minutes

Cooking Time:
8 minutes

Serving:
4

INGREDIENTS

- 454g chicken tender, cut into 5cm pieces
- 1 package dry ranch salad dressing mix
- 2 tbsp flour
- 1 egg, beaten
- 106g bread crumbs
- Olive oil cooking spray
- Parsley for garnishing

DIRECTIONS

1. Add the chicken and ranch seasoning to a bowl, then toss to coat. Allow the chicken to stand for 10 minutes.
2. Place flour, egg, and bread crumbs on different shallow plates.
3. Coat the chicken pieces with flour, dip them in the egg, and then coat them with bread crumbs.
4. Preheat the air fryer to 198°C and grease the air fryer basket with cooking spray.
5. Arrange the chicken pieces in the air fryer basket without overlapping.
6. Spritz the chicken nuggets with cooking spray.
7. Air fry the nuggets for 8 minutes, turning them halfway through cooking.
8. Garnish the nuggets with parsley and serve while hot.

 Nutrition-Per Serving: Calories: 244Kcal, Total Fat: 4g, Carbs: 25g, Protein: 31g

 Variation: Melted butter can be used in place of the egg.

---

10. Air Fryer Turkey Croquettes

Preparation Time:
20 minutes

Cooking Time:
10 minutes

Serving:
6

INGREDIENTS

- 182g potatoes, mashed
- 60g parmesan cheese, grated
- 56gswiss cheese, shredded
- 1 finely chopped shallot

- 2 tbsp fresh rosemary, minced
- 1 tbsp fresh sage, minced
- ½ tbsp salt
- ¼ tbsp pepper
- 83g cooked turkey, chopped
- 1 egg
- 2 tbsp water
- 106g bread crumbs
- Butter-flavoured cooking spray
- Sour cream

DIRECTIONS

1. Preheat the air fryer to 176°C.
2. Mix the potatoes, cheeses, shallot, rosemary, sage, salt, and pepper in a bowl.
3. Stir the turkey into the potato mixture.
4. Make 2 ½ cm patties from the turkey mixture.
5. In a separate bowl, whisk the egg and water.
6. Place the bread crumbs in a different bowl.
7. Dip the croquettes in the egg mixture, then coat them with the bread crumbs.
8. Place the croquettes in the air fryer in a single layer and mist them with cooking spray.
9. Cook the croquettes for 10 minutes, flipping them halfway through cooking.
10. Serve with sour cream.

 Nutrition-Per Serving: Calories: 322Kcal, Total Fat: 12g, Carbs: 21g, Protein: 29g

 Variation: Dried sage leaves can be used instead of fresh sage.

---

11. Air Fryer Sesame Chicken Thighs

Preparation Time:
5 minutes

Cooking Time:
15 minutes

Serving:
4

INGREDIENTS

- 2 tbsp sesame oil
- 2 tbsp soy sauce
- 1 tbsp honey
- 1 tbsp sriracha sauce
- 1 tbsp rice vinegar
- 907g chicken thighs
- 1 chopped green onion
- 2 tbsp sesame seeds, toasted

DIRECTIONS

1. Mix sesame oil, Soy sauce, honey, sriracha, and vinegar in a bowl.
2. Stir the chicken into the marinade and refrigerate for 30 minutes.

3. Preheat the air fryer to 204°C.
4. Drain the marinade and transfer the chicken to an air fryer basket.
5. Cook the chicken thigh for 15 minutes, flipping them after 5 minutes.
6. Place the chicken thighs and garnish with green onion and sesame seeds.
7. Serve and enjoy.

 Nutrition-Per Serving: Calories: 485Kcal, Total Fat: 33g, Carbs: 7g, Protein: 40g

 Variation: Sesame oil can be replaced with olive oil.

12. Air Fryer Bacon Wrapped Stuffed Chicken

Preparation Time:
15 minutes

Cooking Time:
30 minutes

Serving:
4

INGREDIENTS

- 2 chicken breasts
- 112g spinach
- 60g cream cheese
- 30g parmesan cheese, shredded
- 2 tbsp chopped jalapeno peppers
- 1 tbsp black pepper
- ½ tbsp salt
- 6 bacon slices
- 4 tbsp cajun seasoning

DIRECTIONS

1. Cut the chicken breast into halves, then pound them into 1cm.
2. Mix the spinach, cream cheese, parmesan, jalapeno, pepper, and salt in a bowl.
3. Spread the spinach mixture over the chicken breasts.
4. Roll the chicken breast so that the filling remains inside.
5. Rub the chicken with Cajun seasoning.
6. Wrap each chicken with three bacon slices, then place in an air fryer basket.
7. Set the chicken to air fry at 177°C for 30 minutes.
8. Serve and enjoy.

 Nutrition-Per Serving: Calories: 357Kcal, Total Fat: 24g, Carbs: 3g, Protein: 34g

 Variation: De-boned chicken thighs can be used in place of chicken breast.

13. Air Fryer Turkey Stuffed Peppers

Preparation Time:
15 minutes

Cooking Time:
15 minutes

Serving:
3

INGREDIENTS

- Cooking spray
- 3 red bell pepper
- 1 tbsp olive oil
- 347g ground turkey
- 68g brown rice, cooked
- 27g bread crumbs
- 180g low-sodium marinara sauce
- 3 tbsp finely chopped parsley
- ¼ tbsp ground pepper
- 13g parmesan cheese, grated
- 56g part-skim mozzarella cheese, shredded
- Parsley for garnishing

DIRECTIONS

1. Preheat the air fryer to 176°C and spray the air fryer basket with cooking spray.
2. Cut off the pepper tops and reserve them. Deseed the peppers, then set them aside.
3. Heat oil in a skillet over medium heat.
4. Brown the turkey in the skillet for about 4 minutes.
5. Stir in rice and bread crumbs to the turkey and cook for 1 minute. Remove the turkey from heat.
6. Stir in the marinara, parsley, pepper, and parmesan to the turkey mixture.
7. Divide the turkey mixture among the bell pepper.
8. Cover the bell pepper with reserved pepper tops and place them in the air fryer basket.
9. Cook the stuffed peppers for 8 minutes.
10. Remove the pepper tops and sprinkle mozzarella over the peppers.
11. Cook the stuffed peppers for 2 minutes.
12. Sprinkle the peppers with parsley and serve.

 Nutrition-Per Serving: Calories: 407Kcal, Total Fat: 21g, Carbs: 26g, Protein: 29g

 Variation: Green peppers can be used instead of red bell peppers.

---

14. Air Fryer Buffalo Chicken Casserole

Preparation Time:
10 minutes

Cooking Time:
15 minutes

Serving:
4

INGREDIENTS

- 500g rotisserie chicken, shredded
- 58g chopped onion
- 36g cream
- 59ml hot wing sauce
- 60g blue cheese, crumbled
- 64g cream cheese, diced
- Salt and black pepper to taste
- 3g green scallions, chopped

DIRECTIONS

1. Preheat the air fryer to 176ºC and coat a baking dish with cooking spray.
2. Mix all the ingredients in a bowl until they are well combined.
3. Transfer the chicken mixture to the baking dish.
4. Place the baking dish in an air fryer and cook for 15 minutes.
5. Remove the dish from the air fryer and cover with foil for 3 minutes.
6. Garnish the chicken casserole with green onions, then serve.

 Nutrition-Per Serving: Calories: 348Kcal, Total Fat: 22g, Carbs: 3g, Protein: 34g

 Variation: Hot wing sauce can be replaced with sriracha sauce.

CHAPTER 8

AIR FRYER BEEF, PORK, AND LAMB RECIPES

1. Air Fryer Herbed Lamb Chops

Preparation Time: 1 hr 5 minutes

Cooking Time: 7 minutes

Serving: 4

INGREDIENTS

- 1 tbsp rosemary
- 1 tbsp thyme
- 1 tbsp oregano
- 1 tbsp salt
- 1 tbsp coriander
- 2 tbsp olive oil
- 2 tbsp lemon juice
- 454g lamb chops

DIRECTIONS

1. Add all the ingredients except the lamb to a resealable bag and shake to mix.
2. Add the lamb chops to the bag and shake to coat, then refrigerate for 1 hour.
3. Preheat the air fryer to 198ºC.
4. Place the lamb chops in the air fryer and cook for 7 minutes. Flip the lamb chops after 3 minutes of cooking.
5. Plate the lamb chops and serve.

 Nutrition-Per Serving: Calories: 414Kcal, Total Fat: 37g, Carbs: 1g, Protein: 19g

 Variation: Favorite seasoning can be used.

---

2. Air Fryer Lamb Meatballs

Preparation Time: 5 minutes

Cooking Time: 12 minutes

Serving: 4

INGREDIENTS

- 454g ground lamb
- 1 tbsp ground cumin
- 2 tbsp granulated onion
- 2 tbsp fresh parsley
- ¼ tbsp ground cinnamon
- Salt and black pepper

- Cooking spray

DIRECTIONS

1. In a bowl, thoroughly mix the lamb, cumin, onion, parsley, cinnamon, salt, and black pepper until well combined.
2. Make 2 ½ cm balls from the lamb mixture.
3. Lightly mist the meatballs with cooking spray, then place them in an air fryer basket.
4. Air fry the meatballs at 176°C for 15 minutes shaking the basket halfway through cooking.
5. Serve and enjoy.

 Nutrition-Per Serving: Calories: 328Kcal, Total Fat: 22g, Carbs: 1g, Protein: 27g

 Variation: Dried parsley can be used instead of fresh parsley

---

3. Parmesan Air Fryer Pork Chops

Preparation Time:
5 minutes

Cooking Time:
10 minutes

Serving:
4

INGREDIENTS

- 60g grated parmesan
- 1 tbsp salt
- 1 tbsp smoked paprika
- ½ tbsp dried mustard powder
- ½ tbsp garlic powder
- ½ tbsp ground black pepper
- 4 pork chops, boneless
- 1 tbsp avocado oil
- Parsley

DIRECTIONS

1. Preheat the air fryer to 190°C.
2. Mix the parmesan, salt, paprika, mustard powder, garlic powder, and pepper in a bowl.
3. Rub the pork chops with oil, then coat them with the parmesan mixture.
4. Transfer the pork to an air fryer basket.
5. Cook the pork chops for 10 minutes, flipping them halfway through cooking.
6. Allow the pork chops to cool for 5 minutes.
7. Serve the pork chops with parsley.

Nutrition-Per Serving: Calories: 310Kcal, Total Fat: 13g, Carbs: 3g, Protein: 41g

 Variation: Favorite cheese may be used.

4. Air Fryer Pork Chops and Broccoli

Preparation Time:
5 minutes

Cooking Time:
10 minutes

Serving:
2

INGREDIENTS

- 2 tbsp avocado oil
- ½ tbsp paprika
- ½ tbsp onion powder
- ½ tbsp garlic powder
- 2 minced garlic cloves
- 1 tbsp salt
- 177g broccoli florets
- 42g pork chops, bone-in
- 2 tbsp flavoured butter

DIRECTIONS

1. Preheat the air fryer to 176°C.
2. Mix the oil, paprika, onion powder, garlic powder, garlic cloves, and salt in a bowl.
3. Rub the pork chops with the seasoning mixture.
4. Transfer the pork chops to an air fryer basket and cook for 5 minutes.
5. Flip the pork chops and add the broccoli.
6. Cook the pork chops and broccoli for 5 minutes, stirring them after 3 minutes.
7. Serve the pork chops while hot with a dollop of butter.

 Nutrition-Per Serving: Calories: 483Kcal, Total Fat: 30g, Carbs: 12g, Protein: 41g

 Variation: zucchini can be used instead of broccoli.

5. Air Fryer Beef Steak and Mushroom

Preparation Time:
10 minutes

Cooking Time:
15 minutes

Serving:
4

INGREDIENTS

- 454g steak, cubed
- 230g mushrooms
- 2 tbsp melted butter
- 1 tbsp Worcestershire sauce
- ½ tbsp garlic powder
- Salt and black pepper to taste
- Minced parsley

DIRECTIONS

1. In a bowl, mix all the ingredients until they are well combined.
2. Preheat the air fryer to 204°C.
3. Add the steak and mushroom to an air fryer basket.
4. Cook the steak for 15 minutes, shaking the basket three times during the cooking.
5. Garnish the steak and mushroom with parsley and serve.

 Nutrition-Per Serving: Calories: 609Kcal, Total Fat: 35g, Carbs: 9g, Protein: 68g

 Variation: the mushroom can be replaced with a vegetable of your preference.

6. Air Fryer Beef Steak Wrapped Asparagus

Preparation Time:
10 minutes

Cooking Time:
10 minutes

Serving:
6

INGREDIENTS

- 4 tbsp balsamic vinegar
- 4 tbsp olive oil
- 1 garlic clove, crushed
- 1 tbsp salt
- 454g asparagus, trimmed
- 680g beef flank steak, thinly sliced
- 12 grape tomatoes, halved
- Olive oil cooking spray

DIRECTIONS

1. Mix the vinegar, oil, garlic, and salt in a bowl.
2. Place three asparagus on one slice of steak and roll it up.
3. Repeat the process for all the asparagus.
4. Place the wrapped asparagus and tomatoes in the air fryer basket.
5. Brush the wrapped asparagus and tomatoes with the vinegar mixture and

cooking spray.
6. Preheat the air fryer to 198°C.
7. Cook the steak for 1o minutes.
8. Serve and enjoy.

 Nutrition-Per Serving: Calories: 432Kcal, Total Fat: 29g, Carbs: 6g, Protein: 34g

 Variation: Balsamic vinegar can be replaced with apple cider vinegar.

7. Pecan Crusted Air Fryer Pork Chops

Preparation Time:
10 minutes

Cooking Time:
12 minutes

Serving:
6

INGREDIENTS

- 125g pecan pieces
- 46g arrowroot
- 2 tbsp Italian seasoning
- 1 tbsp onion powder
- 1 tbsp garlic powder
- ¼ tbsp salt
- 1 egg

- 1 tbsp dijon mustard
- 1 tbsp water
- 2 garlic cloves
- Six pork chops, boneless and trimmed off the fat
- Parsley for garnishing

DIRECTIONS

1. Preheat the air fryer to 204°C.
2. Mix the pecan, arrowroot, Italian seasoning, onion powder, garlic powder, salt, egg, Dijon, water, and garlic in a bowl.
3. Coat both sides of the pork chops with the pecan mixture and transfer them to an air fryer basket.
4. Cook the pork for 12 minutes, flipping them after 7 minutes.
5. Garnish the pork chops with parsley and serve.

 Nutrition-Per Serving: Calories: 361Kcal, Total Fat: 16g, Carbs: 8g, Protein: 43g

 Variation: Arrowroot can be replaced with corn starch.

8. Air Fryer Roast Lamb Rack with Lemon

Crust

Preparation Time:
15 minutes

Cooking Time:
30 minutes

Serving:
4

INGREDIENTS

- 794g rack of lamb
- Salt and black pepper to taste
- 53g breadcrumbs
- 1 tbsp garlic clove, grated
- 1 tbsp cumin seeds
- 1 tbsp ground cumin
- 1 tbsp oil
- ¼ lemon rinds, grated
- 1 egg, beaten

DIRECTIONS

1. Preheat the air fryer to 100°C.
2. Season the rack of lamb with salt and pepper, then set aside.
3. Mix the bread crumbs, garlic, cumin seeds, ground cumin, oil, and lemon rinds in a bowl.
4. Place the egg on a shallow plate.
5. Dip the rack of lamb in the egg, then coat with the bread crumbs mixture.
6. Place the lamb in the air fryer basket and cook for 25 minutes.
7. Raise the air fryer temperature to 200°C and cook the lamb for an additional 5 minutes.
8. Allow the lamb to stand for 10 minutes, then serve.

 Nutrition-Per Serving: Calories: 400Kcal, Total Fat: 24g, Carbs: 4g, Protein: 44g

 Variation: Bread crumbs can be replaced with oatmeal.

---

9. Air Fryer Mint Lamb with Toasted Hazelnuts and peas

Preparation Time:	Cooking Time:	Serving:
5 minutes	35 minutes	4

INGREDIENTS

- 33g hazelnuts
- 335g shoulder of lamb
- 1 tbsp hazelnut oil
- Salt and black pepper to taste
- 2 tbsp freshly chopped mint leaves
- 34g frozen peas
- 78ml water
- 118ml white wine vinegar
- Mint leaves for topping

DIRECTIONS

1. Air fry the hazelnuts at 160°C for 10 minutes.
2. Mix the lamb, hazelnut oil, salt, and pepper in a bowl.
3. Add the mint to one side of the air fryer, followed by the lamb, then the hazelnuts.
4. Add peas to the other side of the air fryer.
5. Pour water and vinegar over the hazelnuts and peas and air fry at 160°C for 25 minutes.
6. Plate the lamb hazelnuts and peas, then top with mint.
7. Serve and enjoy.

 Nutrition-Per Serving: Calories: 380Kcal, Total Fat: 27g, Carbs: 3g, Protein: 34g

 Variation: White wine vinegar can be replaced with apple cider vinegar.

---

10. Air Fryer Pork and Pineapple Kabobs

Preparation Time:
5 minutes

Cooking Time:
10 minutes

Serving:
4

INGREDIENTS

- Two boneless pork chops, cut into 5cm chunks
- 1 pineapple, peeled and cut into 5 cm chunks
- 1 tbsp fresh parsley, chopped
- 4 skewers

DIRECTIONS

1. Thread the skewers by alternating the pork chops and pineapple.
2. Preheat the air fryer to 176ºC.
3. Cook the kabobs for 10 minutes.
4. Sprinkle the kabobs with parsley and serve.

 Nutrition-Per Serving: Calories: 155Kcal, Total Fat: 3g, Carbs: 10g, Protein: 21g

 Variation: Additional seasoning may be used if desired.

1. Air Fryer Cheesecake

Preparation Time:
15 minutes

Cooking Time:
34 minutes

Serving:
12

INGREDIENTS

- 90g biscuits
- 74ml melted butter
- 396g caster sugar
- 737g feta cheese
- 3 eggs, beaten
- 59ml Greek yoghurt
- 1 tbsp vanilla essence
- Cheesecake crust

DIRECTIONS

1. Pulse the biscuits in a blender until fine crumbs are formed.
2. Mix the butter and biscuit crumbs in a bowl.
3. Add the sugar and cheese to a bowl, then mix with a hand mixer until the mixture gets fluffy.
4. Add the eggs, Greek yoghurt, vanilla, and butter mixture to the cheese mixture. Mix using the hand mixer.
5. Transfer the cheesecake filling to a cheesecake crust.
6. Air fry the cheesecake at 161°C for 30 minutes.
7. Allow the cake to cool for 30 minutes in the air fryer.
8. Cool the cheesecake in the refrigerator for additional 6 hours.
9. Serve and enjoy.

 Nutrition-Per Serving: Calories: 447Kcal, Total Fat: 28g, Carbs: 39g, Protein: 6g

 Variation: feta cheese can be replaced with any favourite soft cheese.

---

2. Air Fryer Chocolate Cupcakes

Preparation Time:
10 minutes

Cooking Time:
12 minutes

Serving:
12

INGREDIENTS

- Cooking spray
- 76g unsweetened cocoa powder
- 118 ml hot water
- 100g sugar
- 59ml vegetable oil
- 118ml milk

- 1 egg, beaten
- 1 tbsp vanilla extract
- 125g flour
- ¾ tbsp baking powder
- ¾ tbsp baking soda
- ½ tbsp salt

For the Chocolate Buttercream:

- 8 tbsp softened butter
- 242g powdered sugar
- 3 tbsp cocoa powder

- Pinch of salt
- ¼ tbsp vanilla extract
- 4 tbsp milk

DIRECTIONS

1. Preheat the air fryer to 310ºC and spray the silicone cupcake holders with cooking spray.
2. Whisk cocoa and water in a bowl until the powder is completely dissolved.
3. Add sugar, oil, milk, egg, and vanilla extract into the cocoa water.
4. Sift flour, baking powder, baking soda, and salt over the cocoa mixture, then mix until well combined.
5. Pour the batter into the cupcake holders and transfer them to an air fryer basket.
6. Cook the cupcakes for 12 minutes.
7. Transfer the cupcakes to a cooling rack and allow them to cool completely.
8. Meanwhile, add the butter, sugar, cocoa powder, salt, and vanilla extract to a bowl and mix using a hand mixer.
9. Gradually add milk to the butter mixture until your preferred consistency is achieved.
10. Spread the buttercream on the cupcake and serve.

 Nutrition-Per Serving: Calories: 278Kcal, Total Fat: 12g, Carbs: 40g, Protein: 4g

 Variation: Milk cream can be used instead of milk.

3. Air Fryer Chocolate Chip Cookies

Preparation Time:
10 minutes

Cooking Time:
5 minutes

Serving:
6

INGREDIENTS

- 84g all-purpose flour
- ¼ tbsp baking soda
- ⅛ tbsp salt
- 64g brown sugar
- 57g unsalted butter
- 2 tbsp white sugar
- 1 egg yolk
- ½ tbsp vanilla extract
- 85g semi-sweet chocolate chips.

DIRECTIONS

1. Preheat the air fryer to 176°C.
2. In a bowl, mix the flour, baking soda, and salt.
3. Add the brown sugar, butter, white sugar, egg, and vanilla extract to a separate bowl.
4. Stir in the flour mixture to the butter mixture until the dough is well combined.
5. Add the chocolate chips to the dough and mix.
6. Scoop 2 spoonfuls of the dough, roll them into balls and then flatten them into cookies.
7. Place the cookies in the air fryer and cook them for 5 minutes.
8. Transfer the cookies to a cooling rack and allow them to cool completely.
9. Serve and enjoy.

 Nutrition-Per Serving: Calories: 268Kcal, Total Fat: 16g, Carbs: 34g, Protein: 4g

 Variation: Bread flour can be used instead of all-purpose flour.

---

4. Air Fryer Chocolate Cake

Preparation Time:
10 minutes

Cooking Time:
15 minutes

Serving:
4

INGREDIENTS

- Cooking spray
- 49g white sugar

- 3 ½ tbsp softened butter
- 1 egg, beaten
- 1 tbsp apricot jam
- 6 tbsp all-purpose flour
- 1 tbsp unsweetened cocoa chips
- Salt to taste

DIRECTIONS

1. Preheat the air fryer to 159ºC and spray a small pan with cooking spray.
2. Add sugar and butter to a bowl and mix using an electric mixer.
3. Add the egg and jam to the butter mixture and mix.
4. Sift the flour, cocoa chips, and salt over the butter mixture and thoroughly mix.
5. Pour all the batter into the pan and level with a spoon.
6. Cook the cake for 15 minutes.
7. Allow the cake to cool, then serve.

 Nutrition-Per Serving: Calories: 380Kcal, Total Fat: 27g, Carbs: 3g, Protein: 34g

 Variation: Strawberry jam can be used instead of apricot jam.

5. Air Fryer Apple Fritters

Preparation Time:
10 minutes

Cooking Time:
7 minutes

Serving:
6

INGREDIENTS

- 125g all-purpose flour
- 2 tbsp sugar
- 1 tbsp baking powder
- ½ tbsp salt
- ½ tbsp ground cinnamon
- ¼ tbsp ground nutmeg
- 1 egg, beaten
- 78ml milk
- 2 tbsp butter, melted
- ½ tbsp lemon juice
- 2 apples, diced

For the Cinnamon Glaze:

- 60gconfectioners sugar
- 2 tbsp milk
- ½ tbsp ground cinnamon
- Pinch of salt

DIRECTIONS

1. Mix the flour, sugar, baking powder, salt, cinnamon, and nutmeg in a bowl.
2. Whisk the egg, milk, butter, and lemon juice in a different bowl.

3. Stir in the flour mixture into the egg mixture until well combined.
4. Fold the apple into the batter.
5. Scoop two spoonfuls of the batter and roll into the fritters.
6. Preheat the air fryer to 187°C.
7. Place the apple fritters in the air fryer basket and cook for 7 minutes.
8. Meanwhile, mix all the cinnamon glaze ingredients in a bowl.
9. Transfer the apple fritters to a wire rack and drizzle the cinnamon glaze on top.
10. Serve and enjoy.

 Nutrition-Per Serving: Calories: 100Kcal, Total Fat: 3g, Carbs: 19g, Protein: 2g

 Variation: Nutmeg can be replaced with mace.

6. Air Fryer Apple Wedges

Preparation Time:
10 minutes

Cooking Time:
5 minutes

Serving:
6

INGREDIENTS

- 106g graham cracker crumbs
- 49g sugar
- 1 tbsp ground cinnamon
- 125g flour
- 3 eggs, beaten
- 3 apples, sliced into wedges
- Caramel sauce

DIRECTIONS

1. Preheat the air fryer to 193°C.
2. Mix graham crackers, crumbs, sugar, and cinnamon in a bowl.
3. Place the flour and egg in 2 different bowls.
4. Dip the apple wedges in the flour, the egg, and the graham crackers crumbs mixture.
5. Place the apple wedges in the air fryer and cook them for 5 minutes.
6. Serve the apple wedges with caramel sauce.

 Nutrition-Per Serving: Calories: 237Kcal, Total Fat: 4g, Carbs: 43g, Protein: 5g

 Variation: Graham crackers crumbs can be substituted with pretzels.

7. Air Fryer Ube Glazed Donuts

Preparation Time:
5 minutes

Cooking Time:
6 minutes

Serving:
8

INGREDIENTS

- 195g powdered sugar
- 2 tbsp 2% milk
- ½ tbsp Ube extract
- ½ tbsp vanilla extract
- 454g flaky layers Biscuits

DIRECTIONS

1. Preheat the air fryer to 175ºCand spray the air fryer basket with cooking spray.
2. Mix powdered sugar, milk, Ube extract, and vanilla extract until well combined.
3. Place the biscuits on a flat surface and make holes at the centre using a 2 ½ cm cookie cutter.
4. Place the doughnuts in the air fryer and cook them for 6 minutes. Flip the doughnut after 3 minutes.
5. Place the doughnuts on a cooling rack and drizzle Ube glaze over.
6. Allow the doughnuts to cool, then serve.

 Nutrition-Per Serving: Calories: 236Kcal, Total Fat: 7g, Carbs: 27g, Protein: 3g

 Variation: 2% milk can be replaced with almond milk.

---

8. Air Fried Oreo

Preparation Time:
5 minutes

Cooking Time:
5 minutes

Serving:
8

INGREDIENTS

- 1 package of Pillsbury crescent rolls
- Powdered sugar
- 8 oreo cookies

DIRECTIONS

1. Spread the crescent roll on a flat surface.
2. Cut the dough into 8 pieces.
3. Place an oreo cookie at the centre of the dough.
4. Stretch and fold the corners of the crescent dough to cover the oreo cookie.
5. Preheat the air fryer to 160°C.
6. Place the Oreos in the air fryer basket and cook them for 5 minutes.
7. Remove the Oreos from the air fryer and dust them with powdered sugar.
8. Let the Oreos cool, then serve.

 Nutrition-Per Serving: Calories: 172Kcal, Total Fat: 4g, Carbs: 32g, Protein: 3g

 Variation: Crescent dough sheets can be used instead of Pillsbury crescent rolls.

---

1. Air Fryer Lava Cakes

Preparation Time:
10 minutes

Cooking Time:
10 minutes

Serving:
2

INGREDIENTS

- Cooking spray
- 85g semi-sweet chocolate chips
- 4 tbsp butter
- 2 eggs, beaten

- 1 tbsp vanilla extract
- ¼ tbsp salt
- 3 tbsp all-purpose flour
- 60g powdered sugar

For the Nutella Filling:

- 2 tbsp Nutella
- 1 tbsp softened butter

- 1 tbsp powdered

DIRECTIONS

1. Preheat the air fryer to 185°Cand spray the ramekins with cooking spray.
2. Add chocolate chips and butter to a bowl, then melt them in the microwave.
3. Stir the eggs, vanilla, salt, flour, and powdered sugar into the butter mixture.
4. Mix the Nutella filling ingredients in a separate bowl until they are well combined.
5. Fill the ramekins with the half-full batter and a Nutella filling at the centre. Cover the Nutella filling with the remaining batter.
6. Place the lava cakes in an air fryer and cook them for 10 minutes.
7. Remove the cakes from the air fryer and flip them over a plate.
8. Allow the cake to cool for 5 minutes, then serve.

 Nutrition-Per Serving: Calories: 776Kcal, Total Fat: 50g, Carbs: 77g, Protein: 10g

 Variation: maple syrup can be used instead of vanilla extract.

---

2. Air Fryer Rice

Preparation Time:
5 minutes

Cooking Time:
16 minutes

Serving:
2

INGREDIENTS

- 2 tbsp soy sauce
- 2 tbsp sriracha sauce
- 500g cooked rice
- 1 tbsp sesame oil
- 1 tbsp water

- 2 tbsp vegetable oil
- Salt and black pepper to taste
- 1 egg, beaten
- 130g peas and carrot

DIRECTIONS

1. Preheat the air fryer to 175ºC.
2. Whisk the soy sauce and sriracha sauce in a bowl, then set aside.
3. Mix the rice, sesame oil, water, vegetable oil, salt, and pepper in a separate bowl.
4. Transfer the rice mixture to a cake pan and place it in the air fryer basket.
5. Cook the rice for 10 minutes stirring halfway through the cooking time.
6. Pour the egg over the rice and cook for 4 minutes.
7. Stir the peas and carrots into the rice, then cook for 2 minutes.
8. Plate the rice and pour the sauce over it.
9. Serve and enjoy.

 Nutrition–Per Serving: Calories: 392Kcal, Total Fat: 15g, Carbs: 55g, Protein: 11g

 Variation: Favorite sauces can be used.

3. Air Fryer Mashed Potato Balls

Preparation Time:
10 minutes

Cooking Time:
12 minutes

Serving:
2

INGREDIENTS

- 26g bread crumbs

- ½ tbsp parmesan cheese, grated

- ¼ tbsp dried parsley
- ⅛ tbsp garlic powder
- ⅛ tbsp black pepper
- ⅛ tbsp salt
- ⅛ cup aquafaba
- 1 tbsp nutritional yeast
- 250g cold mashed potatoes
- Olive oil spray
- For garnishing: grated parmesan cheese and scallions

DIRECTIONS

1. Mix the bread crumbs, parmesan, parsley, garlic powder, pepper, and salt in a bowl.
2. Place the aquafaba and the yeast on 2 different bowls.
3. Scoop 2 spoonfuls of the mashed potatoes and roll them into balls.
4. Coat the balls with yeast, dip them in the aquafaba and coat them with the bread crumbs mixture.
5. Preheat the air fryer to 195°C and grease the air fryer basket with cooking spray.
6. Place the potato balls in the air fryer basket and spritz them with cooking spray.
7. Cook the potato balls for 12 minutes, shaking the basket three times during the cooking.
8. Garnish the potato balls with parmesan and scallions, then serve.

Nutrition-Per Serving: Calories: 95Kcal, Total Fat: 1g, Carbs: 18g, Protein: 5g

Variation: Parmesan cheese can be replaced with favourite cheese.

4. Air Fryer Mac and Cheese

Preparation Time:
20 minutes

Cooking Time:
6 minutes

Serving:
2

INGREDIENTS

- 216g box macaroni and cheese
- 2 bacon slices
- 88g broccoli florets
- 1 egg
- 78g shredded cheddar cheese
- 26g French fried onions

DIRECTIONS

1. Cook the macaroni and cheese according to the packaging directions.
2. Meanwhile, cook the bacon in a skillet over medium heat for 10 minutes.

3. Stir in the broccoli to the mac and cheese during the last 2 minutes of cooking.
4. Cut the bacon into small pieces and mix with the egg in a bowl.
5. Stir in the bacon mixture to the mac and cheese mixture.
6. Preheat the air fryer to 200°C and spray the muffin cups with cooking spray.
7. Fill the muffin cups with two spoonfuls of the mac and cheese mixture, then top with cheddar cheese and fried onions.
8. Cook the mac and cheese bites for 8 minutes.
9. Let the mac and cheese bite cool for 3 minutes, then use tongs to remove them from the cups.
10. Serve and enjoy.

 Nutrition–Per Serving: Calories: 55Kcal, Total Fat: 3g, Carbs: 6g, Protein: 3g

Variation: Broccoli can be replaced with preferred veggies.

---

5. Air Fryer Blackened Chicken Breast

Preparation Time: 10 minutes

Cooking Time: 20 minutes

Serving: 2

INGREDIENTS

- 2 tbsp paprika
- 1 tbsp ground thyme
- 1 tbsp cumin
- ½ tbsp cayenne pepper
- ½ tbsp onion powder
- ½ tbsp black pepper
- ¼ tbsp salt
- 2 tbsp vegetable oil
- Two chicken breast halves, skinless and boneless
- Cooked rice and broccoli
- Parsley for topping

DIRECTIONS

1. Mix paprika, thyme, cumin, cayenne pepper, onion powder, black pepper, and salt in a bowl.
2. Coat the chicken breast with oil, then rub them with the seasoning mixture.
3. Allow the chicken to marinate for 5 minutes.
4. Preheat the air fryer to 180°C
5. Place the chicken breast in the air fryer basket and cook for 20 minutes. Flip the chicken after 10 minutes of cooking.
6. Serve the chicken with cooked rice and broccoli and top with parsley.

Nutrition-Per Serving: Calories: 432Kcal, Total Fat: 10g, Carbs: 3g, Protein: 79g

 Variation: The seasonings may be adjusted to fit your preference.

6. Air Fryer Lemon Pepper Shrimp

Preparation Time:
5 minutes

Cooking Time:
6 minutes

Serving:
2

INGREDIENTS

- 1 tbsp olive oil
- 1 lemon juice
- 1 tbsp lemon pepper
- ¼ tbsp paprika
- ¼ tbsp garlic powder
- 340g shrimp, peeled and deveined
- 1 lemon, sliced
- Parsley for topping

DIRECTIONS

1. Preheat the air fryer to 200ºC
2. Mix olive oil, lemon juice, lemon pepper, paprika, and garlic powder in a bowl until well combined.
3. Add the shrimp to the seasoning mixture and toss to coat.
4. Place the shrimp in an air fryer basket and cook for 6 minutes.
5. Serve the shrimp with lemon slices and sprinkle some parsley.

 Nutrition-Per Serving: Calories: 215Kcal, Total Fat: 9g, Carbs: 13g, Protein: 29g

 Variation: Favorite additional seasonings may be used.

7. Air Fryer Salmon cake with Sriracha Mayo

Preparation Time:
15 minutes

Cooking Time:
8 minutes

Serving:
2

INGREDIENTS

For Sriracha Mayo:
- 27g mayonnaise
- ½ tbsp sriracha

For the Salmon Cakes:
- 227g salmon fillets, skinless
- 24g almond flour
- 1 egg, beaten
- ¾ tbsp old bay seasoning
- 1 green onion, chopped
- Cooking spray

DIRECTIONS

1. In a bowl, prepare the sriracha mayo by whisking mayonnaise and sriracha. Refrigerate until ready to use.
2. Add one tablespoon of sriracha mayo, salmon, almond flour, egg, seasoning, and ¾ of the onion to a food processor and pulse until they are well combined.
3. Make 4 patties from the salmon mixture and refrigerate them for 15 minutes.
4. Preheat the air fryer to 195°C and spray the air fryer basket with cooking spray.
5. Spritz the salmon patties with cooking spray and place them in the air fryer basket.
6. Cook the cakes for 8 minutes.
7. Serve the salmon with the remaining sriracha mayo and green onions.

 Nutrition-Per Serving: Calories: 340Kcal, Total Fat: 25g, Carbs: 4g, Protein: 26g

 Variation: Red onions can be used instead of green onions.

---

8. Air Fryer Taco Hot Dogs

Preparation Time:
5 minutes

Cooking Time:
9 minutes

Serving:
2

INGREDIENTS

- 2 hot dogs
- 1 tbsp taco seasoning mix
- 2 hot dog buns
- 50g guacamole
- 4 tbsp salsa
- 6 slices of pickled jalapeno
- 1 lemon, halved

DIRECTIONS

1. Preheat the air fryer to 195°C.
2. Make 5 cuts on each hot dog, then rub them with the taco seasoning.
3. Place the hot dogs in the air fryer basket and cook them for 5 minutes.
4. Place the hot dogs in the buns and cook for 4 minutes.
5. Top the hot dog with guacamole, salsa, and jalapeno.
6. Serve the taco hot dogs with lemon slices.

 Nutrition-Per Serving: Calories: 380Kcal, Total Fat: 27g, Carbs: 3g, Protein: 34g

 Variation: Favorite toppings can be used.

---

1. Air Fryer Pork Chops with Brussels Sprouts

Preparation Time:
10 minutes

Cooking Time:
10 minutes

Serving:
1

INGREDIENTS

- 120g pork chops, bone-in
- Cooking spray
- ⅛ tbsp salt
- ½ tbsp black pepper
- 1 tbsp olive oil
- 1 tbsp maple syrup
- 1 tbsp Dijon mustard
- 113g Brussels sprouts

DIRECTIONS

1. Mist the pork chops with cooking spray and season them with salt and ¼ tablespoon of pepper.
2. Whisk oil, maple syrup, mustard, and remaining pepper in a bowl.
3. Add the Brussels to the Dijon mixture and toss to coat.
4. Preheat the air fryer to 200ºC
5. Place the pork chops on one side of the air fryer basket and the Brussels on the other.
6. Cook the pork chops for 10 minutes.
7. Serve and enjoy.

 Nutrition-Per Serving: Calories: 337Kcal, Total Fat: 11g, Carbs: 21g, Protein: 39g

 Variation: Dijon mustard can be replaced with mayonnaise.

---

2. Air Fryer Smoky Pork Tenderloin with Butternut

Squash

Preparation Time:
10 minutes

Cooking Time:
17 minutes

Serving:
1

INGREDIENTS

- 113g pork tenderloin
- ½ tbsp smoked paprika
- Salt and black pepper to taste
- ⅛ tbsp ground cumin
- ½ tbsp canola oil
- 52g butternut squash
- 30ml cider vinegar
- ¾ tbsp honey
- ¼ tbsp Dijon mustard
- 1 thyme sprig
- ¼ tbsp unsalted butter, melted

DIRECTIONS

1. Preheat the air fryer to 200°C.
2. Sprinkle the pork with paprika, salt, pepper, and cumin, then rub to coat.
3. Heat ¼ tablespoon oil in a skillet over medium heat, then brown the pork on both sides for 4 minutes.
4. Add the butternut and remaining oil to a bowl and toss to coat.
5. Air fry the butternut for 5 minutes.
6. Stir the pork into the butternut and cook for 8 minutes.
7. Remove the pork and butternut from the air fryer and let stand for 5 minutes.
8. Meanwhile, mix the vinegar, honey, mustard, thyme, and salt in a saucepan.
9. Cook the sauce over medium heat until thickened.
10. Stir the butter into the sauce and remove it from heat. Discard the thyme sprig.
11. Plate the pork and butternut, then drizzle the sauce.
12. Serve and enjoy.

 Nutrition-Per Serving: Calories: 390Kcal, Total Fat: 13g, Carbs: 44g, Protein: 25g

 Variation: Dijon mustard can be replaced with mayonnaise.

---

3. Air Fried Sesame-Crusted Cod with Snap Peas

Preparation Time:
10 minutes

Cooking Time:
16 minutes

Serving:
1

INGREDIENTS

- 1 cod fillet
- ½ tbsp vegetable oil
- Salt and black pepper to taste
- 1 tbsp butter
- ½ tbsp sesame seeds
- 45gsugar snap peas
- 1 garlic clove, sliced
- 2 orange wedges

DIRECTIONS

1. Preheat the air fryer to 200°C and grease the air fryer basket with vegetable oil.
2. Dry the salmon with a paper towel, then season it with salt and pepper.
3. In a bowl, mix the butter and sesame seeds.
4. In a separate bowl, add the peas, garlic, and ½ of the butter mixture and toss to mix.
5. Place the peas in an air fryer and cook for 10 minutes. Shake the basket two times during the cooking.
6. Transfer the snap peas to a bowl. Keep the snap peas warm.
7. Brush the fillet with the remaining butter mixture, then place it in the air fryer.
8. Cook the fillet for 6 minutes
9. Serve the fillet with the peas and orange wedges.

 Nutrition-Per Serving: Calories: 364Kcal, Total Fat: 15g, Carbs: 23g, Protein: 31g

 Variation: Vegetable oil can be replaced with cooking spray.

---

4. Garlic Butter Air Fryer Mushrooms

Preparation Time:	Cooking Time:	Serving:
5 minutes	6 minutes	1

INGREDIENTS

- 113g mushrooms
- ¼ tbsp olive oil
- ½ tbsp soy sauce
- Black pepper to taste
- ¼ tbsp garlic butter
- 1 tbsp parsley

DIRECTIONS

1. Preheat the air fryer to 200°C.
2. Add mushroom, oil, soy sauce, and pepper to a bowl and toss to coat.
3. Place the mushroom in an air fryer basket and cook for 6 minutes. Shake the basket after 4 minutes of cooking.
4. Transfer the mushroom to a bowl.
5. Stir in butter and parsley to the mushroom until well mixed.
6. Serve while warm.

 Nutrition-Per Serving: Calories: 83Kcal, Total Fat: 7g, Carbs: 4g, Protein: 3g

Variation: Favourite seasonings can be used.

---

5. Air Fryer Maple Sage Squash

Preparation Time:	Cooking Time:	Serving:
10 minutes	12 minutes	1

INGREDIENTS

- 57g butternut squash, peeled and cut into 2 ½ cm pieces
- 1 tbsp olive oil
- ½ tbsp salt
- A handful of sage leaves
- ½ tbsp maple syrup
- 2 tbsp pomegranate seeds

DIRECTIONS

1. Add the squash, ½ tablespoon oil, and salt to a bowl and toss to coat.
2. Preheat the air fryer to 190°C.

3. Place the squash in an air fryer basket and cook for 7 minutes.
4. Meanwhile, rub the sage with the remaining oil.
5. Stir in the sage to the squash and cook for 5 minutes.
6. Transfer the squash to a bowl, drizzle with maple syrup, and then toss to coat.
7. Plate the squash and sprinkle pomegranate seed over.
8. Serve and enjoy.

 Nutrition-Per Serving: Calories: 685Kcal, Total Fat: 63g, Carbs: 33g, Protein: 3g

 Variation: Preferred squash can be used.

6. Air Fryer Veggies

Preparation Time:
15 minutes

Cooking Time:
8 minutes

Serving:
1

INGREDIENTS

- 30g zucchini, diced
- 30g yellow squash, diced
- 30g mushroom, diced
- 1 red onion, diced
- 30g sweet red pepper, diced
- 1 tbsp vegetable oil
- Salt and black pepper to taste
- 1 tbsp balsamic vinegar

DIRECTIONS

1. Preheat the air fryer to 180°C.
2. Add all the ingredients to a bowl and toss to mix.
3. Place the veggies in the air fryer basket.
4. Cook the veggies for 8 minutes, shaking the basket after 4 minutes of cooking.
5. Serve and enjoy.

 Nutrition-Per Serving: Calories: 155Kcal, Total Fat: 14g, Carbs: 8g, Protein: 2g

 Variation: Seasoning can be done to suit your preference.

7. Air Fryer Brussels Sprouts with Bacon and Maple Syrup

Preparation Time:
10 minutes

Cooking Time:
10 minutes

Serving:
1

INGREDIENTS

- 2 tbsp avocado oil
- 2 tbsp maple syrup
- 1 tbsp apple cider vinegar
- Salt and black pepper
- 113g Brussels sprouts, trimmed
- One slice of bacon, cut into small pieces

DIRECTIONS

1. Add oil, maple syrup, vinegar, salt, and pepper to a bowl and mix.
2. Stir in the Brussel sprouts and bacon to the marinade.
3. Preheat the air fryer to 175°C.
4. Transfer the Brussels sprouts and bacon to an air fryer.
5. Cook the Brussels and bacon for 10 minutes stirring halfway through cooking.
6. Serve and enjoy.

 Nutrition-Per Serving: Calories: 528Kcal, Total Fat: 39g, Carbs: 42g, Protein: 8g

 Variation: Red wine vinegar can be used in place of apple cider vinegar

8. Air Fryer Cheese Stuffed Mushroom

Preparation Time:
5 minutes

Cooking Time:
8 minutes

Serving:
1

INGREDIENTS

- 31g fresh Portobello mushroom
- 28g cream cheese
- 1 tbsp parmesan cheese, shredded
- ½ tbsp sharp cheddar cheese, shredded
- ½ tbsp white cheddar cheese, shredded
- 1 tbsp Worcestershire sauce
- 1 garlic clove, minced
- Salt and black pepper to taste
- Parsley for garnishing

DIRECTIONS

1. Cut off the mushroom stem and remove much of the mushroom flesh.
2. Mix cream cheese, parmesan, cheddar cheeses, Worcestershire sauce, garlic, salt, and pepper in a bowl.
3. Preheat the air fryer to 185°C.
4. Stuff the mushrooms with the cheese mixture and place them in the air fryer basket.
5. Cook the stuffed mushroom for 8 minutes.
6. Allow the mushrooms to cool.
7. Sprinkle parsley over the mushrooms and serve.

 Nutrition-Per Serving: Calories: 116Kcal, Total Fat: 7g, Carbs: 3g, Protein: 8g

Variation: Preferred cheeses can be used

9. Air Fryer Salmon and Asparagus

Preparation Time:
5 minutes

Cooking Time:
8 minutes

Serving:
1

INGREDIENTS

- ¾ tbsp lemon juice
- ½ tbsp olive oil
- 1 tbsp fresh dill, chopped
- 1 tbsp fresh parsley, chopped
- Salt and pepper to taste
- 1 salmon filet
- 1 bunch asparagus

DIRECTIONS

1. Mix lemon juice, olive oil, dill, parsley, salt, and pepper in a bowl.
2. Coat the salmon with ¾ dill mixture.
3. Stir the asparagus into the remaining dill mixture.
4. Preheat the air fryer to 200°C.
5. Place the asparagus at the bottom of the air fryer basket and layer the salmon on top.
6. Cook the salmon for 8 minutes.
7. Plate and serve.

 Nutrition-Per Serving: Calories: 391Kcal, Total Fat: 20g, Carbs: 9g, Protein: 48g

 Variation: Preferred herbs can be used.

10. Air Fryer Meatloaf

Preparation Time:
10 minutes

Cooking Time:
25 minutes

Serving:
1

INGREDIENTS

- Cooking spray
- 113g lean ground beef
- 1 egg, beaten
- 1 tbsp bread crumbs
- 1 finely chopped onion
- ¼ tbsp chopped thyme
- Salt and black pepper
- 1 small mushroom, chopped
- 2 tbsp buffalo wings sauce

DIRECTIONS

1. Preheat the air fryer to 198°C and spray a baking pan with cooking spray.
2. Mix the beef, egg, breadcrumbs, onion, thyme, salt, and pepper in a bowl.
3. Transfer the beef mixture to the pan and level the top with a spoon.
4. Press the mushroom into the beef mixture and spritz the top with cooking spray.
5. Transfer the pan to the air fryer basket and cook for 25 minutes.
6. Allow the meatloaf to cool, then slice it.
7. Serve the meatloaf with buffalo wings sauce.

 Nutrition-Per Serving: Calories: 296Kcal, Total Fat: 19g, Carbs: 6g, Protein: 25g

 Variation: Breadcrumbs may be substituted with oatmeal.

AIR FRYER COOKING CHART

Vegetables in the Air Fryer

Asparagus	5 Mins	400°F 204°C	(sliced 1-inch)
Beest	40 Mins	400°F 204°C	(whole)
Broccoli	6 Mins	400'F 204°C	(florets)
Brussels Sprouts	15 Mins	380"F 193°C	(halved)
Carrots	15 Mins	380"F 193°C	(sliced½-inch)
Cauliflower	12 Mins	400°F 204°C	(florets)
Com on the cob	6 Mins	390"F 199°C	
Eggplant	15 Mins	400°F 204°C	(1½-inch cubes)
Fennel	15 Mins	370'F 188°C	(quartered)
Green Beans	5 Mins	400°F 204°C	
Kale leaves	12 Mins	250'F 121°C	
Mushrooms	5 Mins	400F' 204°C	(sliced ¼-Inch)
Onions	10 Mins	400'F 204°C	(pearl)
Parsnips	15 Mins	380"F 193°C	(½-inchchunks)
Peppers	15 Mins	400°F 204°C	(1-inchchunks)
Potatoes	15 Mins	400'F 204°C	(small baby, 1.5 lbs)
Potatoes	12 Mins	400°F 204°C	(1-inchchunks)
Potatoes	40 Mins	400'F 204°C	(baked whole)

Squash	12 Mins	400'F 204°C	(½-inchchunks)
Sweet Potato	30 to 35 Mins	380"F 193°C	(baked)
Tomatoe	4 Mins	400'F 204°C	(scherry)
Tomatoes	10 Mins	-18°C	(halves)
Zucchini	12 Mins	350'F 177°C	(½-inchsticks)

Chicken in the Air Fryer

Breast's bone	25 Mins	370'F 188°C	(1.25lbs.)
Breasts, boneless	12 Mins	380"F 193°C	(4 oz.)
Drumsticks	20 Mins	370F' 188°C	(2.5 lbs.)
Thighs, bone In	22 Mins	380"F 193°C	(2 lbs.)
Thighs, boneless	18 to 20 Mins	380"F 193°C	(1.5 lbs.)
Legs, bone In	30 Mins	380"F 193°C	(1.75lbs.)
Wings	12 Mins	400'F 204°C	(2 lbs.)
Game Hen	20 Mins	390"F 199°C	(halved- 2lbs.)
Whole Chicken	75 Mins	360'F 182°C	(6.5 lbs.)
Tenders	8 to 10 Mins	360'F 182°C	

Beef in the Air Fryer

Burger	16 to 20 Mins	370' F 188°C	(4 oz.)
Flie! Mignon	18 Mins	400°F 204°C	(8 oz.)
Flank Steak	12 Mins	400'F 204°C	(1.5 lbs.)
London Broil	20 to 28 Mins	400'F 204°C	(2 lbs.)
Meatballs	7 Mins	380"F 193°C	1-inch}
Meatballs	10 Mins	380"F 193°C	(3-inch)
Ribeye, bone In	10 to 15 Mins	400'F 204°C	1-inch, 8 oz.}
Sirloin steaks	9 to 14 Mins	400'F 204°C	1-inch,12 oz.}
Beef Eye Round Roast	45 to 55 Mins	390"F 199°C	(4lbs.)

Pork and Lamb in the Air Fryer

Loin	55 Mins	360°F 182°C	(2 lbs.)
Pork Chops, bone In	12 Mins	400°F 204°C	(1-inch, 6.5 oz.)
Tenderloin	15 Mins	370°F 188°C	(1lb.)
Bacon	5 to 7 Mins	400°F 204°C	(regular)
Bacon	6 to10 Mins	400°F 204°C	thick cut}
Sausages	15 Mins	380°F 193°C	
Lamb LoinChops	8 to 12 Mins	400°F 204°C	(1-inch thick)
Rack of lamb	22 Mins	380°F 193°C	(1.5 - 2lbs.)

Fish and Seafood in the Air Fryer

Calamari	4 Mins	400°F 204°C	8 oz.}
Fish Fillet	10 Mins	400°F 204°C	1-inch, 8 oz.}
Salmon, fillet	12 Mins	380°F 193°C	(6oz.)
Swordfish steak	10 Mins	400°F 204°C	
Tunasteak	7 to 10 Mins	400°F 204°C	
Scallops	5 to 7 Mins	400°F 204°C	
Shrtmp	5 Mins	400°F 204°C	

Frozen Foods in the Air Fryer

OnionRings	8 Mins	400°F 204°C	(12 oz.)
Thin French Fries	14 Mins	400°F 204°C	(20oz.)
Thick French Fries	18 Mins	400°F 204°C	17oz.}
Mozzarella Sticks	8 Mins	400°F 204°C	(11oz.)
Pot stickers	8 Mins	400°F 204°C	(10 oz.)
Fish Sticks	10 Mins	400°F 204°C	{10 OZ.}
Fish Fillets	14 Mins	400°F 204°C	(½-inch, 1oz.)
Chicken Nuggets	10 Mins	400°F 204°C	12oz.}
Breaded Shrimp	9 Mins	400°F 204°C	

Sweet Foods in the Air Fryer

Chocolate Brownie Cookies	40-45 minutes	300°F 150°C
Chocolate Chip Cookies	15 minutes	180 ° C 360 ° F
Hash Browns	11 minutes	200° C 390° F
Sugar Cookies	10 minutes	160°C 320°F
Cinnamon Rolls	9 minutes	180 ° C 360 ° F
Dougnuts	4 to 5 minutes	180 ° C 360 ° F
Churros	10 minutes	195 °C 380°F
Apple pie	30 minutes	160°C 320°F
Banana Bread	45 minutes	160° C 320 ° F
Apple chips	8 minutes	200° C 390° F

Snacks in the Air Fryer

Hotdogs	6 minutes	180 ° C 360 ° F
Baked potatoes	40 minutes	400°F 204°C
Empanadas	7 minutes	400°F 204°C
Pizza	9 minutes	180 ° C 360 ° F
Potato Chips	15 minutes	180 ° C 360 ° F
French Fries	10 minutes	180 ° C 360 ° F
McCain Superfries Shoestring	10 minutes	180 ° C 360 ° F

Fresh Cut Fries	30 minutes	180 ° C 360 ° F
Frozen french fries	19 minutes	400°F 200°C
Sweet Potato Fries	10 minutes	400°F 204°C
Potato Wedges	30 minutes	400°F 204°C
Crumbed Chicken Tenderloins	12 minutes	350°F 175°C

AIR FRYER CONVERSION TABLE

VOLUME EQUIVALENT (LIQUID)

us standard	us standard Oz	metric(approx.)
2 tbsp	1 fl.oz	30 ml
¼ cup	2 fl.oz	60 ml
½ cup	4 fl.oz	120 ml
1 cup	8 fl.oz	240 ml
1 1/2 cup	12 fl.oz	355 ml
2 cups/ 1 pint	36 fl.oz	475 ml
4 cups/ 1 quart	32 fl.oz	1 L
1 gallon	128 fl.oz	4 L

TEMPERATURES

FAHRENHEIT (F)	CELCIUS (C)
250	120
300	150
325	165
350	180
375	190
400	200
425	220
450	230

VOLUME EQUIVALENT (DRY)

US STANDARD	METRIC (Approx.)
1/8 tbsp	0.5 ml
¼ tbsp	1 ml
½ tbsp	2 ml
¾ tbsp	5 ml
1 tbsp	15 ml
1 Tbsp	59 ml
1/8 cup	79 ml
¼ cup	119 ml
½ cup	156 ml
¾ cup	177 ml
1 cup	235 ml
2 cups/ 1 pint	475 ml
3 cups	700 ml
4 cups	1 L
½ gallon	2 L
1 gallon	4 L

WEIGHT EQUIVALENT

US STANDARD	METRIC (Approx.)
½ ounce	15g
1 ounce	30g
2 ounce	60g
4 ounce	115g
8 ounce	225g
12 ounce	340g
16 ounce/ 1 pound	455g

BONUS!

Thanks! Find your gift here!

An extensive collection of air fryer meals to have even more Ideas, or make a gift. Send the Pdf to friends and family with a single Click on Whatsapp or Social Network. Enjoy!

Printed in Great Britain
by Amazon

12318484R00059